Winning Marketing Strategies Using Generative AI

Steve Swartz,

To one of the brightest business
leaders I have encountered.
Thanks for you help and support
when I was with Hearst.

Best,

Bay

Winning Marketing Strategies Using Generative AI

Gary W. Randazzo

Leader in applied, concise business books

First published in 2024 by
Business Expert Press, LLC
222 East 46th Street, New York, NY 10017
www.businessexpertpress.com

ISBN-13: 978-1-63742-730-9 (paperback)
ISBN-13: 978-1-63742-731-6 (e-book)

Business Expert Press Marketing Collection

First edition: 2024

10 9 8 7 6 5 4 3 2 1

Description

Using generative AI to develop winning marketing strategies uses the mission, vision, objective, situation analysis (market research), strategy, tactics, and execution structure (MVOSSTE) to guide market strategists through the market strategy-building process. Generative AI is used as a tool throughout the process to provide the marketing strategist or executive with a broader array of options for each phase of MVOSSTE.

Examples throughout the book show how AI can be used to develop mission and vision statements, develop research programs to identify target markets, develop organizational structures, develop metrics that support organizational goals, and create operating procedures. Each example is footnoted with the prompt that resulted in the AI response.

The use of AI with the MVOSSTE structure can provide students, strategists, and executives with a clear roadmap to creating effective marketing strategies.

Contents

Introduction

A Process to Address Business Challenges—Mission, Vision, Objective, Situation Analysis, Strategy, Tactics, and Execution (MVOSSTE).

If you are starting a business or have an existing business, you need a process that is consistent and provides a roadmap to reaching business and financial goals. The process I will introduce in this book is **MVOSSTE**, which stands for mission, vision, objective, situation analysis, strategy, tactics, and execution. Using this approach, organizations can find new markets, set pricing, determine logistical needs, determine the best approach to creating value, and assuring sustainable growth.

Generative AI can be used with this process to expand creativity and innovation for more comprehensive business approaches. In each of the areas discussed in the book, AI can be asked to give solutions for mission statements, core competencies, and so on. As the book approaches new and existing company examples, AI will be asked to provide input.

The reader should know that generative AI is a tool, not a solution. AI is naive in that it does not understand your business, industry, or personal objectives unless you provide that information.

The reader should also understand that the data used by AI might have errors and may cause inaccurate responses. The reader is advised to verify AI responses through other resources.

This book will use examples of business start-ups and established businesses. AI will be employed to generate ideas and approaches to each step of the MVOSSTE approach.

Choosing a carefully considered prompt or directive to AI can help provide quality responses. Throughout this book, each AI-generated response is footnoted with the prompt given to AI. Review of the footnotes should give the reader an idea of how to direct the AI response to more precisely provide the requested information.

CHAPTER 1

Mission

Overview

This chapter focuses on the purpose of a mission statement and how AI can be used to give a strategist assistance in creating a mission statement that endures over time.

Mission

Mission statement requires an understanding of why the business exists. This is not how an organization will make money but rather, the reason for it to exist. Coca-Cola, for example, exists *"to refresh the world, bring moments of optimism and create value and make a difference."*[1] Notice there is no mention of products in this statement.

A mission statement helps identify the scope of an organization's activities. It is important to make the mission statement broad enough to allow growth opportunities but not so broad that the organization doesn't have a clear path forward.

For Coca-Cola, the mission statement is very broad but still fits their core product and provides opportunities to expand.

Theodore Levitt,[2] in his article, said that railroads defined their business as railroads but could have more broadly defined the business as that of transportation. This might have allowed railroads to avoid some of the downturns caused by the advent of cargo aircraft and trucks.

Clayton Christensen[3] in his book, *The Innovator's Solution*, talks about the job to be done.

The mission statement should define the job to be done rather than a product or service.

Here are two examples of mission statements and how AI might help in creating them.

New Organization Example

For a new company, having invented a new fingernail clipper might be tempted to say its mission was *"to provide quality nail care."* Using the help of AI, a better mission statement using Levitt's *Marketing Myopia* article as a guide might be:

> *Anticipating and Satisfying Customer Needs Beyond Nail Groom-*
> *ing: [Company Name] embraces Theodore Levitt's Marketing*
> *Myopia philosophy to craft a mission that extends beyond the mere*
> *provision of nail clippers. Our mission is to be a customer-cen-*
> *tric organization, dedicated to anticipating and satisfying evolving*
> *grooming needs comprehensively.*
>
> *With Levitt's insight as our guide, we commit to continually*
> *understanding the broader landscape of personal care. Our mission*
> *is to offer not just nail clippers but a suite of innovative grooming*
> *solutions that align with contemporary lifestyles. By maintaining*
> *a forward-thinking perspective and adapting to changing customer*
> *demands, we aspire to ensure enduring relevance and value for our*
> *customers.*
>
> *Grounded in the principles of Marketing Myopia, we pledge*
> *to cultivate a customer-focused culture within [Company Name],*
> *where every product and service embodies a commitment to exceeding*
> *customer expectations. Our mission is to evolve with our customers,*
> *demonstrating agility, innovation, and an unwavering dedication to*
> *enhancing their overall grooming experience. In doing so, we aim not*
> *only to sell products but to establish lasting connections and contribute*
> *meaningfully to the holistic well-being of our customers.*[*]

This mission statement describes the job someone using nail clippers wants done. An organization looking for long-term success needs to identify the job customers want done.

---

[*]This was provided by ChatGPT responding to the prompt: "Using Theodore Levitt's Article, Marketing Myopia, create a mission statement for the nail clipper company."

Existing Organization Example

An existing organization may not have a formal mission statement or may have drifted from the original intent of the organization's founders. In these cases, to employ the MVOSSTE (Mission, Vision, Objective, Situation Analysis, Strategy, Tactics, Execution) approach, it will be necessary to determine the job the organization is trying to perform.

Newspapers today face tremendous challenges and may feel like they are on the brink of becoming extinct. A typical newspaper might have a mission statement such as:

> *To inform, engage, and empower our community through credible journalism. [Newspaper Name] is committed to delivering timely and accurate news coverage, insightful analysis, and diverse perspectives. Our mission is to serve as a reliable source of information that fosters an informed and enlightened society. We strive to uphold the values of journalistic integrity, objectivity, and community service, acting as a watchdog, storyteller, and catalyst for positive change in the communities we serve.*[†]

While this allows the newspaper the ability to move to different platforms for dissemination, it may not describe the job the public wants. Today a significant group of individuals are likely to get their news and information from social media. Social media may have information that is not vetted and provide users with incorrect information. Perhaps a solution would be to define a broader mission for the newspaper using Christensen's "Job to be done" framework, the mission statement might look like:

> *Enabling Informed Lives by Fulfilling Evolving Informational Needs: [Newspaper Name] draws inspiration from Clayton Christensen's 'The Job to be Done' framework to redefine our mission in today's dynamic media landscape. Our commitment is to understand and fulfill the ever-changing informational needs of our audience, recognizing that*

[†] This was provided by ChatGPT responding to the prompt "What is the mission of a newspaper?"

the "job" our customers hire us for extends beyond traditional news delivery.

In line with Christensen's principles, our mission is to serve as a catalyst for individual empowerment and community engagement. We aim to provide not just news but curated, insightful, and diverse content that serves the specific "jobs" our readers are hiring us for— whether it's staying informed, gaining perspective, or connecting with their community.

By embracing innovation and leveraging emerging technologies, we pledge to adapt our offerings to meet the evolving "jobs" of our readers in the digital age. Our mission is to be a trusted guide in their information-seeking journey, utilizing a multi-platform approach to deliver relevant, timely, and thought-provoking content. Through this, we strive to contribute to the enrichment of lives, fostering an informed and connected society in the contemporary media environment.[‡]

This second mission statement more closely aligns with the job individual information seekers want done as evidenced by how they currently get their information—through social media and streaming news outlets. As you might suspect, this creates a challenge in defining the products the newspaper will have to offer, what the workforce will look like, how products and services will need to be measured for success, and so on.

Summary

The mission statement can provide a guiding light for an organization. It should be well thought out and consider the more enduring view of having an overall purpose not just creating a product or service. AI can provide assistance in developing a mission statement but should not be viewed as providing the only approach. A good mission statement guides the development of the vision of how the organization will create value.

[‡] This was provided by ChatGPT responding to the prompt "Using Clayton Christensen's 'the job to be done' discussion in the Innovator's Solution, create a mission statement for a newspaper in today's media environment."

CHAPTER 2

Vision

Overview

In the previous chapter, a mission statement was created to provide a purpose for the organization but did not speak to specific products or services that would be offered. The vision statement gives the organization an opportunity to describe how it will create value. This may be through a product or service. It is important to remember that the vision must be in alignment with the mission. Rather than a specific product or service, the strategist should identify an approach that allows adjustments for changes in the market and customer needs. AI can assist in giving some options for a vision statement.

Vision

Whether it is new or existing, an organization will need to identify how it will create value for the customers, the organization, and its collaborators. This comes in the vision statement which provides a clear vector for the mission to be carried out.

A vision statement should articulate how the organization will create value for itself, the customers, and the collaborators. Coca-Cola has the following vision statement:

> Our vision is to craft the brands and choice of drinks that people love, to refresh them in body and spirit. And done in ways that create a more sustainable business and better-shared future that makes a difference in people's lives, communities, and our planet.[1]

This statement says they will create value through the offering of beverages that will provide a sustainable financial and social (employees, customers, and collaborators) framework.

Adopting this vision will require planning for the products offered or to be offered, the price that can be charged that will provide sustainable income for the company and be willingly paid by the customer, the required logistics to get the products to the customer and the communications needed to make the customer aware of the products and the product benefits. This is the price, place, product, and promotion that most marketing strategies are built around.

An organization should consider how it will create value. One approach is to compete with other similar organizations in the current markets or it could consider a vision based on the Disruptive Innovation theories set forth by Clayton Christensen or Blue Ocean Strategies introduced by Chan Kim and Renee Mauborgne. Christensen's theories posit that market leaders can be displaced by providing overserved customers (customers not needing all of the attributes offered by the market leaders in the industry) with "good enough" products. Blue Ocean Strategies focuses on business approaches that create new markets to which potential competitors cannot respond. A strategist using Blue Ocean Strategies would likely create A Blue Ocean Canvas which depicts attributes of organizations that provide similar products to identify opportunities in the marketplace. Below is a Blue Ocean Canvas that a regional newspaper might use to identify market opportunities (Figure 2.1).

As you can see, newspapers have an edge on local news, preprint distribution, and vetted content. If the newspaper can market a product using formats to attract social media users built around local news and vetted content, a new market might be created to which social media outlets might not be able to respond. Adding the preprint distribution ability tied to social media would make it very difficult for competitors to respond.

New Organization Example

A new company may have only one product but may have opportunities to increase product or service offerings in the future. A vision statement employing tenets of Clayton Christensen's *Disruptive Innovation* for the nail clipper company mentioned in the mission section might be:

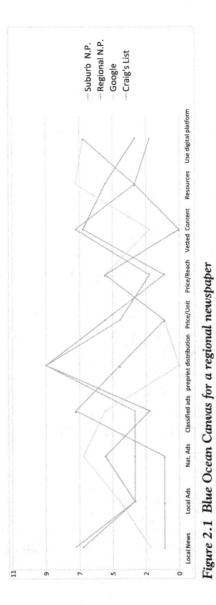

Figure 2.1 Blue Ocean Canvas for a regional newspaper

Empowering the Underserved with Affordable Excellence: [Company Name] envisions a future where disruptive innovation, inspired by Clayton Christensen's theories on "over served" customers, propels us to redefine the personal grooming landscape. Our vision is to create immense value for customers, the company, and collaborators by addressing the needs of those who may not require the extra features offered by market leaders.

Understanding the unique preferences of the "over served" customers, we commit to delivering nail care solutions that are not only high-quality but also affordable, foregoing unnecessary extras. By embracing a "good enough" philosophy, we aim to provide a cost-effective alternative without compromising on essential functionality.

In our pursuit of excellence, we seek collaborative partnerships to broaden our insights and ensure our offerings resonate with a diverse customer base. Our vision is to be a catalyst for positive change in the industry, where every customer can access reliable and affordable grooming tools. Through this approach, [Company Name] aims to create a win-win scenario, providing value to customers, ensuring sustainable growth for the company, and fostering collaborative success with our valued partners.[*]

Existing Organization Example

Using the news organization mentioned earlier, a vision statement that intended to employ social media strategies with the conventional approach of newspapers might be:

---

[*]ChatGPT responding to the prompt "Christensen defines over served customers as those that don't need the product extras offered by market leaders and might be good prospects for a 'good enough' product that is cheaper and doesn't have all of the attributes offered by market leaders. Restate the vision statement for the nail clipper company using this definition while creating value for the customer, company and collaborators."

Empowering Informed Communities: [Newspaper Name] envisions a future where dynamic journalism, integrated with strategic social media engagement, transforms the way information is shared and consumed. Our vision is to create significant value for customers, the company, and collaborators by not only delivering quality news but also fostering meaningful connections through innovative social media strategies.

Understanding the evolving media landscape, we commit to delivering news content that is not only insightful but also engaging across various social media platforms. By leveraging interactive storytelling, multimedia elements, and real-time updates, we aim to provide an immersive and personalized news experience for our audience.

In our pursuit of connectivity, we seek collaborative partnerships to enhance our social media strategies, ensuring that our content resonates with a diverse and digitally savvy readership. Our vision is to be a trailblazer in the integration of traditional journalism with cutting-edge social media engagement, creating value for readers, ensuring sustainable growth for the company, and fostering collaborative success with our valued partners in the ever-evolving media landscape.[†]

Summary

It is important to develop a vision that fits with the mission statement while finding a way to create value for customers, collaborators, and the company. AI was used to create examples. A strategist may use AI and sit down with others to discuss changes and perhaps provide new prompts for an AI-generated vision. A good vision statement is required to set objectives for the organization.

[†]ChatGPT responding to the prompt "Create a vision statement to create value for the customers, the company and the collaborators for a newspaper that will also engage the audience through social media strategies."

CHAPTER 3

Objective

Overview

After mission and vision statements have been set in place, an objective should be created. The objective has to be in alignment with the mission and vision and it must be measurable. This provides a clear path for an organization to begin considering strategies. AI can be a useful tool in developing such objectives.

Objective

After setting mission and vision statements, an organization should look for an objective that is measurable and achievable within a reasonable amount of time. If an objective does not have a metric to indicate when success has been achieved, the organization can easily be distracted and fail in reaching its intended goals. Objectives that are set too high may result in demoralizing the workforce and most likely will be missed.

New Organization Example

If we continue to use the nail clipper company, an AI-generated objective set for the company might be:

One-Year Measurable Objectives

- **Sales Growth:**
  - *Achieve a 15 percent increase in sales compared to the previous year.*

- o *Introduce at least two new nail care products to diversify the product portfolio.*
- **Customer Engagement:**
  - o *Increase customer engagement on social media platforms by 20 percent through interactive campaigns and promotions.*
  - o *Gather feedback from customers through surveys and improve product features based on customer preferences.*
- **Market Expansion:**
  - o *Establish distribution partnerships with at least three major retail chains, expanding the availability of products in new geographic locations.*
  - o *Increase online presence by optimizing the company website and exploring partnerships with e-commerce platforms.*
- **Innovation and Quality:**
  - o *Implement at least one product innovation, such as an ergonomic design enhancement or new material application.*
  - o *Conduct quality assurance checks and achieve a 95 percent customer satisfaction rate.*

Five-Year Measurable Objectives

- **Market Leadership:**
  - o *Attain a 25 percent market share in the nail care industry, becoming a recognized leader in quality and innovation.*
  - o *Expand the product line to include grooming solutions beyond nail clippers, capturing a broader segment of the personal care market.*
- **Global Presence:**
  - o *Establish a presence in at least three international markets, adapting products to meet diverse cultural preferences.*
  - o *Implement a robust global marketing strategy to increase brand recognition and preference.*
- **Sustainability Initiatives:**
  - o *Introduce eco-friendly packaging for all products, aligning the company with sustainability goals.*

- Explore partnerships with environmental organizations to support and promote sustainability initiatives.
- **Customer Loyalty Programs:**
  - Implement a customer loyalty program to encourage repeat purchases and referrals.
  - Achieve a 30 percent increase in customer retention rates through personalized offers and exclusive promotions.
- **Collaborations and Partnerships:**
  - Establish collaborations with influencers and beauty experts to enhance brand credibility and reach new audiences.
  - Forge strategic partnerships with complementary hygiene and wellness brands to create bundled products and cross-promotional campaigns.[*]

Existing Organization Example

Continuing with the newspaper organization example, an AI-generated objective focused on attracting users from social media might be:

One-Year Measurable Objectives

- **Digital Transformation:**
  - Increase digital subscriptions by 25 percent through targeted online campaigns and incentives.
  - Enhance the online user experience, achieving a 20 percent reduction in bounce rates and a 15 percent increase in time spent on the website.
- **Social Media Engagement:**
  - Grow social media followership by 30 percent across major platforms.
  - Increase the average engagement rate on social media posts by 20 percent through interactive content and real-time updates.
- **Collaborative Content Partnerships:**

---

[*]ChatGPT responding to the prompt "Using the nail clipper company example, create measurable objectives for one year and five years."

- o *Establish collaborations with at least two influencers or social media personalities to cocreate content and expand audience reach.*
- o *Forge partnerships with local community organizations to feature community-driven content, fostering reader engagement.*
- **Data Analytics and Personalization:**
  - o *Implement data analytics tools to gather insights into reader preferences and behavior.*
  - o *Launch a personalized content recommendation system, achieving a 15 percent increase in user engagement with recommended articles.*

Five-Year Measurable Objectives

- **Global Reach:**
  - o *Expand international readership by 40 percent, targeting specific regions with culturally relevant content.*
  - o *Establish multilingual capabilities to cater to diverse audiences, aligning with the goal of becoming a global news source.*
- **Monetization Strategies:**
  - o *Diversify revenue streams by introducing premium subscription packages and exclusive content for subscribers.*
  - o *Explore e-commerce opportunities through partnerships, such as selling merchandise related to popular news topics.*
- **Innovative Storytelling:**
  - o *Invest in immersive storytelling techniques, such as augmented reality (AR) and virtual reality (VR), for in-depth news experiences.*
  - o *Launch a podcast series featuring in-depth interviews and discussions on trending topics, expanding the brand's content offerings.*
- **Strategic Collaborations:**
  - o *Collaborate with social media platforms to optimize content sharing and increase visibility.*

- o *Establish partnerships with technology companies to explore innovative news delivery methods, such as voice-activated news briefings and AI-driven news summaries.*
- **Community Empowerment:**
  - o *Launch community-driven initiatives, such as citizen journalism programs, to involve readers in news reporting.*
  - o *Establish a foundation or fund to support journalism education and promote media literacy within communities served by the newspaper.[†]*

Summary

Mission, vision, and setting an objective are the foundational steps to creating a strategy that is most likely to provide sustainable value for an organization, its customers, and collaborators. Generative AI can be a useful tool in providing guidance and presenting approaches that might not have been otherwise considered.

All mission, vision, and objective statements need to be reviewed by an organization's staff as to their alignment with the organization, its culture, and capabilities. Using AI as a tool may provide additional options for an organization to consider. AI may also provide output that organizational leaders may not want to pursue.

The strategist must understand that moving forward to the next steps in the MVOSSTE process should not begin until the mission, vision, and objectives are adopted by the organization.

It is important to understand that mission, vision, and objective are critical in establishing a quality strategic plan and understanding the research that will be required to succeed.

[†]ChatGPT responding to the prompt "Create one and five-year objectives for a newspaper with a vision statement to create value for its customers, itself and its collaborators that would use Blue Ocean strategies to attract individuals who use social media as a news source."

CHAPTER 4

Situation Analysis

Overview

Having set a mission, vision, and objective that have been adopted by the organization, it is critical to assess the state of the market, the viability of the objective set, and the hypotheses that support the objective. AI is a useful tool for identifying research requirements, assessing hypotheses, understanding the competencies required, and developing financial analyses.

Situation Analysis

Situation analysis refers to the research that a strategic planner must do to identify an organization's current status, the status of the industry, the identity of the customers, and the ability to craft a strategy to meet the organization's stated objectives.

A strategist has to know if the customers sought provide a market worth pursuing, what products should be offered, what logistics should be used, what communication/advertising programs should be deployed, and what price can be charged that will generate positive financial results.

Knowing the above will require a strategist to understand workforce, financial, and fixed asset requirements, as well as operating procedures needed to successfully deploy a successful strategy.

Additionally, a strategist may want to approach the market with the objective of displacing the market leaders, creating a Blue Ocean where the competition is irrelevant, or creating a niche in the current market configuration.

Any strategy would have to consider the demographics of the target market, the nature of the competition and their approach to the market, the resource requirements to implement a strategy, and the competencies required for the successful execution of the strategy. The next sections will explore these through the lens of the nail clipper company and newspaper organization used in the first chapter.

Identifying Target Market and Size of Market

Identifying who will purchase a product or service can be accomplished through surveys, demographic studies, and census data. Zeroing in on the best market segments requires an understanding of the job to be done and the groups of individuals that need that job done. Generative AI can be helpful, but results should be validated through follow-up surveys and focus groups.

New Organization Example

For the nail clipper company, the AI-generated approach to identifying the research needed to define the target market and size might look like:

To identify the target market and size for a nail clipper company aiming to capture 25 percent of the market using a disruptive innovation strategy, several research steps are crucial. Here's a comprehensive research plan:

1. ***Market Analysis:***
   - ***Current Market Size:***
     - *Conduct a thorough analysis of the current nail clipper market size, including revenue, units sold, and key players.*
   - ***Market Trends:***
     - *Identify trends in the nail care industry, such as preferences for certain designs, materials, or features.*
   - ***Customer Segmentation:***
     - *Segment the market based on demographics, psychographics, and behavior to understand the diverse needs of potential customers.*
2. ***Competitor Analysis:***
   - ***Identify Competitors:***
     - *List and analyze existing nail clipper competitors, noting their market share, strengths, and weaknesses.*

- o ***Product Offerings:***
  - ▪ *Evaluate the features and innovations offered by competitors, understanding the gaps in the market.*
- o ***Customer Reviews and Feedback:***
  - ▪ *Analyze customer reviews and feedback on existing nail clippers to identify pain points and unmet needs.*

3. ***Disruptive Innovation Analysis:***
   - o ***Technology and Material Trends:***
     - ▪ *Investigate emerging technologies and materials relevant to nail care, considering innovations that could disrupt the current market.*
   - o ***User-Centric Design:***
     - ▪ *Explore user-centric design principles to identify ways to improve the user experience with nail clippers.*
   - o ***Affordability and Accessibility:***
     - ▪ *Evaluate strategies for making nail clippers more affordable and accessible to a broader audience.*

4. ***Target Market Identification:***
   - o ***Customer Surveys:***
     - ▪ *Conduct surveys to understand customer preferences, pain points, and willingness to try new nail clipper innovations.*
   - o ***Focus Groups:***
     - ▪ *Organize focus group discussions to gain qualitative insights into consumer behavior and attitudes toward nail care products.*
   - o ***Social Media Listening:***
     - ▪ *Monitor social media platforms for discussions related to nail care and identify trends and preferences.*

5. ***Market Sizing and Forecasting:***
   - o ***Quantitative Surveys:***
     - ▪ *Deploy quantitative surveys to estimate the potential market size for innovative nail clippers.*
   - o ***Regression Analysis:***
     - ▪ *Utilize regression analysis to identify factors influencing the demand for nail clippers and predict future market trends.*

6. ***Regulatory and Compliance Research:***
   - o ***Industry Regulations:***

- *Understand and comply with industry regulations and standards for nail care products.*
  - ○ ***Environmental Impact:***
    - *Investigate sustainability requirements and preferences in the target market to align with eco-friendly trends.*
7. ***Distribution Channel Analysis:***
   - ○ ***Retailer Partnerships:***
     - *Explore potential partnerships with retailers and distributors, understanding their reach and customer base.*
   - ○ ***Online Platforms:***
     - *Analyze the potential of online platforms for selling nail clippers, considering the rise in e-commerce.*
8. ***Pricing Strategy Research:***
   - ○ ***Cost Analysis:***
     - *Conduct a detailed cost analysis of manufacturing, marketing, and distribution to determine a competitive yet profitable pricing strategy.*
   - ○ ***Perceived Value:***
     - *Assess customer perceptions of the value of innovative nail clippers to guide pricing decisions.*
9. ***Marketing and Positioning:***
   - ○ ***Brand Perception:***
     - *Understand how the brand will be perceived in the market and identify key messages for marketing.*
   - ○ ***Communication Channels:***
     - *Identify the most effective communication channels to reach the target audience.*
10. ***Pilot Testing:***
    - ○ ***Prototype Testing:***
      - *Develop prototypes of disruptive nail clippers and conduct pilot testing to gather real-world feedback.*
    - ○ ***Iterative Development:***
      - *Use iterative development based on pilot test results to refine the product.*

By conducting thorough research in these areas, the nail clipper company can gain valuable insights into the target market, customer preferences, and *disruptive opportunities that will guide its strategy to capture 25 percent of the market.**

McKinsey's Hypothesis Tree

To identify specific research that might be needed, it might be useful to use McKinsey Consulting's MECE (mutually exclusive, collectively exhaustive) approach to building a hypothesis tree. This approach requires the strategist to identify the mutually exclusive, collectively exhaustive approaches to a problem or objective. With assistance from AI, the resulting hypothesis tree allows the strategist to pursue options to solve the problem or reach an objective. The marketing strategist can choose among the hypotheses and determine which to pursue. Of course, all hypotheses would have to be tested and proven before implementation.

The hypothesis tree (Figure 4.1) shows the MECE approach in a decision tree format.

Here are a couple of examples of AI-generated hypothesis trees.

New Organization Example

If the main objective for the nail clipper company is to increase sales, a MECE-based hypothesis tree might be:

I. *Increase Sales for the Nail Clipper Company*
   A. *Product-Related Hypotheses*
      1. *Product Innovation*
         a. *Ergonomic Design Improvements*
         b. *New Material Applications*
      2. *Diversification*
         a. *Introduce Complementary Grooming Products*
         b. *Create Bundled Packages*

---

*ChatGPT responding to the prompt "What research would be needed to identify the target market and size for a nail clipper company wishing to capture 25 percent of the nail clipper market using a disruptive innovation strategy."

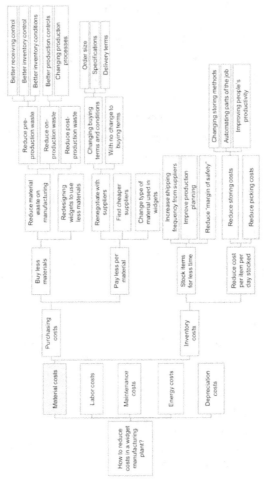

Figure 4.1 Hypothesis tree in decision tree format

    B. *Marketing and Distribution Hypotheses*
       1. *Social Media Engagement*
          a. *Interactive Campaigns*
          b. *Influencer Collaborations*
       2. *Market Expansion*
          a. *Partnerships With Retail Chains*
          b. *Online Presence Optimization*
    C. *Customer Experience Hypotheses*
       1. *Quality Assurance*
          a. *Rigorous Quality Checks*
          b. *Customer Feedback Collection*
       2. *Customer Loyalty*
          a. *Implement Loyalty Program*
          b. *Provide Exclusive Promotions*
    D. *Collaborative Partnerships Hypotheses*
       1. *Industry Collaborations*
          a. *Joint Marketing Efforts*
          b. *Cross-Promotional Campaigns*
       2. *Supplier Collaboration*
          a. *Sustainable and Cost-Effective Material Partnerships*
          b. *Streamlined Supply Chain*
II. *Testing and Analyzing Each Hypothesis*
    A. *Design Experiments*
    B. *Gather Data*
    C. *Analyze Results*
    D. *Iterate and Refine Strategies*[†]

If the strategist were to choose to pursue a strategy built around new material applications under the product innovation approach, a second hypothesis tree could be generated. It might look like:

I. *Increase Sales for the Nail Clipper Company*
    A. *Product-Related Hypotheses*
       1. *Product Innovation*

[†]ChatGPT responding to the prompt "using MECE create a hypothesis tree for the nail clipper company."

a. *Ergonomic Design Improvements*
b. *New Material Applications*
   i. *Test and Evaluate New Materials*
- *Hypothesis: Introducing novel materials will enhance product durability.*
- *Sub-Hypothesis: Conduct material strength tests.*
- *Sub-Hypothesis: Analyze customer feedback on durability.*

   ii. *Eco-friendly Material Introduction*
- *Hypothesis: Incorporating sustainable materials will attract environmentally conscious customers.*
- *Sub-Hypothesis: Source eco-friendly materials.*
- *Sub-Hypothesis: Monitor market response to sustainability initiatives.*

   iii. *Esthetic and Textural Enhancements*
- *Hypothesis: Introducing materials with unique textures or colors will increase product appeal.*
- *Sub-Hypothesis: Conduct consumer surveys on preferred esthetic features.*
- *Sub-Hypothesis: Monitor sales data for new esthetic variants.*[‡]

This would identify research requirements for new material applications.

Each hypothesis shown on the original outline of options could be addressed by creating an additional hypothesis tree for each new approach to be considered. The original list, of course, can be reduced to the options that an organization wants to pursue.

[‡]ChatGPT responding to the prompt "Create a MECE hypothesis tree for new material applications in the above diagram."

Existing Organization Example

For the newspaper wanting to create a Blue Ocean Strategy and target social media users, the AI-generated hypothesis tree might look like:

I. *Blue Ocean Strategy for News Consumption*
   A. *Audience Segmentation*
      1. *Identify Target Audience*
         a. *Hypothesis: Focusing on individuals who primarily use social media for news will create a Blue Ocean.*
            i. *Sub-Hypothesis: Analyze demographic data of social media news consumers.*
            ii. *Sub-Hypothesis: Conduct surveys to understand preferences and behaviors.*
   B. *Content Delivery and Presentation*
      1. *Social Media Integration*
         a. *Hypothesis: Integrating news content seamlessly with social media platforms will attract a larger audience.*
            i. *Sub-Hypothesis: Optimize content for sharing on major social media platforms.*
            ii. *Sub-Hypothesis: Monitor audience engagement metrics on social media.*
   C. *Innovative Storytelling Techniques*
      1. *Multimedia Integration*
         a. *Hypothesis: Introducing multimedia elements will enhance engagement.*
            i. *Sub-Hypothesis: Incorporate videos, infographics, and interactive elements into news stories.*
            ii. *Sub-Hypothesis: Measure audience response to multimedia content.*
   D. *Collaborative Partnerships*
      1. *Influencer Collaborations*
         a. *Hypothesis: Collaborating with social media influencers will expand reach.*
            i. *Sub-Hypothesis: Identify and partner with influencers in relevant niches.*

    ii. *Sub-Hypothesis: Track changes in readership and engagement after collaborations.*

  E. *User-Generated Content*

    1. *Hypothesis: Encouraging user-generated content will foster community engagement.*

     a. *Sub-Hypothesis: Implement platforms for user contributions and feedback.*

     b. *Sub-Hypothesis: Monitor the growth of user-generated content and its impact on engagement.*

  F. *Data-Driven Personalization*

    1. *Hypothesis: Implementing data analytics for personalized content recommendations will enhance user satisfaction.*

     a. *Sub-Hypothesis: Integrate data analytics tools to understand user preferences.*

     b. *Sub-Hypothesis: Track changes in user engagement and satisfaction with personalized content.*

II. *Testing and Analyzing Each Hypothesis*

  A. *Design Experiments*

  B. *Gather Data*

  C. *Analyze Results*[§]

Again, this activity identified the research that could be done to develop a strategy for a newspaper wishing to use the Blue Ocean Strategy approach for attracting social media users.

Core Competencies

After conducting research on the market, it is useful to consider the core competencies that would be needed to carry out the strategy and how these competencies might be acquired. AI can be useful in helping to identify key competencies and how they might be acquired.

[§]ChatGPT responding to the prompt "Create a hypothesis tree for the newspaper wishing to create a Blue Ocean Strategy by focusing on individuals that get their news from social media."

New Organization Example

Using the nail clipper organization pursuing a product innovation strategy under the new material application, the AI-generated core competencies might be:

Implementing a product improvement strategy, specifically focusing on new material applications, requires certain core competencies for the nail clipper company. These competencies are crucial for successfully developing, producing, and marketing innovative nail care products. Here are the core competencies needed:

- *Material Science Expertise:*
  - *Understanding of Materials: In-depth knowledge of various materials, including metals, alloys, and potentially new and innovative materials suitable for nail clipper production.*
  - *Material Testing: Competency in conducting material strength tests, durability assessments, and other relevant testing protocols to ensure the quality of the materials used.*
- *Product Design and Engineering:*
  - *Design Innovation: Ability to innovate and design ergonomic and aesthetically pleasing nail clippers that incorporate new materials seamlessly.*
  - *Prototyping and Testing: Proficiency in prototyping new designs and conducting rigorous testing to ensure functionality, durability, and user-friendliness.*
- *Manufacturing Excellence:*
  - *Production Processes: Competence in implementing efficient manufacturing processes that can accommodate the use of new materials while maintaining product quality and consistency.*
  - *Quality Control: Strong quality control processes to ensure that each nail clipper meets the desired standards.*
- *Market Research and Consumer Insights:*
  - *Understanding Customer Needs: Competency in market research to identify customer preferences, needs, and trends in the grooming industry.*

- o **Consumer Behavior Analysis:** *Ability to analyze consumer behavior and preferences, especially regarding grooming tools and materials.*
- **Innovation Culture:**
  - o **Continuous Learning and Adaptation:** *A company culture that promotes continuous learning and adapts to emerging trends in material science, design, and consumer preferences.*
  - o **Open to Experimentation:** *Willingness to experiment with new ideas, materials, and design concepts to stay ahead of the competition.*
- **Supply Chain Management:**
  - o **Supplier Relationships:** *Establishing and maintaining strong relationships with suppliers, especially those providing innovative materials.*
  - o **Logistics and Distribution:** *Competency in managing logistics and distribution efficiently, ensuring the timely availability of materials and products.*
- **Marketing and Branding:**
  - o **Brand Positioning:** *Ability to position the brand as an innovator and a provider of high-quality grooming products.*
  - o **Marketing Strategies:** *Proficiency in creating and executing marketing strategies that highlight the use of new materials and the benefits they bring to customers.*
- **Regulatory Compliance:**
  - o **Understanding Regulations:** *A clear understanding of regulations and compliance standards related to the use of materials in grooming products.*
  - o **Product Certification:** *Competence in obtaining necessary certifications for new materials and products.*
- **Customer Engagement and Feedback:**
  - o **Customer Service Excellence:** *Providing excellent customer service and engagement to gather feedback and insights on the acceptance and performance of new materials.*
  - o **Iterative Improvement:** *A culture of iterative improvement based on customer feedback and market trends.*
- **Cross-Functional Collaboration:**

- ○ ***Interdepartmental Collaboration:*** *Encouraging collaboration between different departments (R&D, marketing, manufacturing) to ensure seamless integration of new materials into the product.*

By cultivating and leveraging these core competencies, the nail clipper company can successfully execute a product improvement strategy centered around new material applications, driving innovation and customer satisfaction in the grooming industry.[¶]

A new company start-up might not have access to these competencies and might want to find the most cost-effective way of acquiring them. While the executives of the company might have solutions, they might not include some viable alternatives. Here are some AI-generated options to acquire the needed competencies.

Acquiring the necessary competencies for implementing a product improvement strategy focused on new material applications in the most cost-effective way involves a combination of strategies. Here are some approaches:

- ***Internal Training and Development:***
  - ○ *Utilize existing resources within the organization to provide training and development opportunities for employees.*
  - ○ *Offer cross-functional training programs to build skills in areas such as material science, product design, manufacturing processes, and market research.*
  - ○ *Encourage employees to pursue relevant certifications or courses to enhance their expertise.*
- ***Collaboration and Partnerships:***
  - ○ *Form strategic partnerships with academic institutions, research organizations, or industry experts specializing in material science and product design.*

[¶]ChatGPT responding to the prompt "Using the nail clipper company wishing to use new material application under a product improvement strategy, what are the core competencies that would be required?"

- o   *Collaborate with suppliers who can provide expertise and support in the selection and utilization of new materials.*
- o   *Explore codevelopment opportunities with other companies in the grooming industry to share knowledge and resources.*

- **Knowledge Sharing and Networking:**
  - o   *Encourage knowledge sharing among employees through internal workshops, seminars, and forums focused on material science, product innovation, and market trends.*
  - o   *Participate in industry conferences, trade shows, and networking events to stay updated on the latest advancements in material science and connect with potential partners or experts.*

- **Utilization of Online Resources:**
  - o   *Take advantage of online learning platforms and resources that offer courses, webinars, and tutorials on material science, product design, and related topics.*
  - o   *Access open-source materials and research publications to stay informed about the latest developments in material science and product innovation.*

- **Lean and Agile Processes:**
  - o   *Implement lean and agile methodologies to streamline processes and optimize resource utilization.*
  - o   *Focus on prioritizing initiatives that deliver the most value and impact, allowing for efficient allocation of resources toward competency development.*

- **Continuous Improvement Culture:**
  - o   *Foster a culture of continuous improvement where employees are encouraged to experiment, learn from failures, and adapt quickly.*
  - o   *Establish feedback mechanisms to gather insights from employees and stakeholders, enabling iterative refinement of competency-building initiatives.*

- **Outsourcing Noncore Functions:**
  - o   *Consider outsourcing noncore functions or tasks that require specialized expertise, such as material testing or regulatory compliance, to external service providers.*

- o *Evaluate the cost-effectiveness of outsourcing versus building in-house capabilities for specific competencies.*
- **Flexible Talent Acquisition:**
  - o *Opt for flexible talent acquisition strategies such as hiring freelancers, consultants, or part-time specialists for short-term projects or specific expertise needs.*
  - o *Leverage the gig economy and remote work arrangements to access talent pools beyond geographic constraints, potentially reducing costs associated with full-time employment.*

By adopting a strategic and resource-conscious approach to competency acquisition, the nail clipper company can effectively develop the necessary skills and expertise to drive success in implementing its product improvement strategy focused on new material applications.[**]

Talent Acquisition for a News Organization

It is important to note that more questions can be asked to arrive at more specific approaches; for example, identifying approaches to acquiring flexible talent might result in these options:

Flexible talent acquisition involves various options that allow companies to access skills and expertise as needed without the long-term commitments associated with traditional full-time employment. Here are some of the best options for flexible talent acquisition:

- **Freelancers and Independent Contractors:**
  - o *Platforms: Utilize freelancing platforms such as Upwork, Fiverr, and Freelancer to find skilled professionals for short-term projects.*
  - o *Specialized Platforms: Explore industry-specific freelancing platforms that cater to niche skills and expertise.*
- **Consultants:**

[**]ChatGPT responding to the prompt "What is the most cost effective way of acquiring these competencies?"

- o *Industry Experts: Engage consultants who are industry experts in areas like material science, product design, or market research.*
- o *Management Consultants: Hire management consultants for strategic guidance and expertise in implementing organizational changes.*
- **Part-Time Employees:**
  - o *Job Sharing: Consider job-sharing arrangements where two part-time employees share responsibilities traditionally handled by a full-time position.*
  - o *Remote Part-Time Work: Offer remote part-time positions to tap into a broader talent pool and accommodate diverse schedules.*
- **Temporary Staffing Agencies:**
  - o *Contract Staffing: Partner with temporary staffing agencies to fill short-term roles with qualified professionals.*
  - o *Project-Based Staffing: Collaborate with agencies that specialize in project-based staffing for specific skill sets.*
- **Internship Programs:**
  - o *Project-Based Internships: Bring in interns for project-based assignments, allowing them to contribute to specific initiatives.*
  - o *Pipeline for Future Talent: Use internships as a pipeline for identifying potential future full-time employees.*
- **Remote Teams and Outsourcing:**
  - o *Offshore Teams: Consider outsourcing certain functions or tasks to offshore teams for cost-effective solutions.*
  - o *Remote Teams: Build remote teams that can collaborate virtually, providing flexibility for both the company and the talent.*
- **Gig Economy Platforms:**
  - o *Task-Based Platforms: Platforms like TaskRabbit or Gigster allow companies to hire individuals for specific tasks or projects.*
  - o *Skill-Specific Platforms: Explore platforms dedicated to specific skills, such as writing, design, or coding.*
- **Retirees and Industry Veterans:**
  - o *Part-Time Roles: Tap into the expertise of retired professionals who may be interested in part-time or consultancy roles.*

- o *Mentorship Programs: Establish mentorship programs where industry veterans provide guidance and knowledge transfer.*
- **Collaborative Communities:**
  - o *Open Source Communities: Engage with open-source communities where professionals contribute voluntarily, providing a cost-effective way to access expertise.*
  - o *Industry Forums and Groups: Participate in industry-specific forums and groups where professionals share insights and may be available for collaboration.*
- **Flexible Work Platforms:**
  - o *FlexJobs: Utilize platforms like FlexJobs that connect employers with professionals seeking flexible work arrangements.*
  - o *Remote Job Boards: Explore job boards specifically focused on remote and flexible job opportunities.*

When considering flexible talent acquisition, it's essential to align the chosen approach with the specific needs of the company and the nature of the projects or roles. Additionally, effective communication, clear project expectations, and collaboration tools are key to successful engagement with flexible talent.[††]

Breakeven Point

The cost of developing, manufacturing, and delivering a product is crucial to developing a sustainable marketing strategy. It requires an understanding of the cost of making or delivering a product (variable costs) or service as well as the costs of the organization that will occur even if there are no sales of the product or service (fixed costs). These costs can be broken into categories as follows:

- Variable costs:
  - o Material for products;
  - o Labor per unit produced;

[††]ChatGPT responding to the prompt "provide some effective approaches to acquiring flexible talent."

  ○ Shipping costs per unit;

  ○ Marketing costs per unit, such as discounts;

  ○ Any other cost related to the volume of units produced or services delivered.

 • Fixed costs:

  ○ Rent;

  ○ Utilities;

  ○ Debt;

  ○ Depreciation;

  ○ Insurance;

  ○ Administrative and managerial payroll;

  ○ Any other costs that would likely be incurred by the business even if sales are not made.

The price charged for a product or service must be greater than its variable costs. The difference between the price and the variable costs for each product is its markup.

The organization's breakeven point is reached when enough volume of the product has been sold to cover the fixed cost. That is, the markup on each product sold contributes to the fixed cost, and when the fixed cost is covered, the company has reached its breakeven point. Sales above the breakeven point result in a contribution to profit.

The formula for breakeven is simply fixed costs divided by the markup per unit, which yields the sales volume needed to breakeven. So, if a product costs one dollar to produce and sells for two dollars, yielding a one-dollar markup, and fixed costs were one million dollars, then it would be necessary to sell one million units to breakeven.

This is an important research step that allows for the solid development of pricing strategies. Understanding the needed volume will indicate the size of the market that will be needed to be successful.

Newspaper Example

AI can be useful in providing some guidance here. Using the newspaper wishing to attract social media as an example and asking AI to give an estimate of costs might look like the following:

Estimating costs for the initial investment and monthly operating expenses of a social news engagement app or an immersive news ecosystem involves considering various factors across different categories. Please note that these estimates are broad and can vary based on the scale, features, and specific requirements of your product. Additionally, market research and detailed financial planning are recommended for accurate estimations. Here's a general breakdown:

Initial Investment

- ***Development and Technology:***
  - *App Development: $100,000 to $500,000 (depending on complexity and features);*
  - *VR Technology Integration: $50,000 to $200,000;*
  - *AI Algorithms: $30,000 to $100,000;*
  - *Blockchain Integration: $50,000 to $150,000.*
- ***Content Creation:***
  - *Multimedia Production: $50,000 to $200,000;*
  - *Collaboration With Influencers: $20,000 to $100,000.*
- ***Marketing and Launch:***
  - *Branding and Marketing: $50,000 to $150,000;*
  - *Launch Events and Promotions: $30,000 to $100,000.*
- ***Community Engagement:***
  - *Community Platform Development: $20,000 to $80,000;*
  - *User Engagement Initiatives: $10,000 to $50,000.*
- *• **Legal and Compliance:***
  - *Trademark Registration: $5,000 to $20,000;*
  - *Legal Consultation: $10,000 to $30,000.*
- ***Infrastructure and Hosting:***
  - *Cloud Services: $20,000 to $50,000;*
  - *Servers and Hosting: $10,000 to $30,000.*
- ***Miscellaneous:***
  - *Contingency: $20,000 to $50,000;*
  - *Professional Fees (Accounting, Consultation): $10,000 to $30,000.*

Total Estimated Initial Investment: $525,000 to $1,700,000.

Monthly Operating Expenses

- ***Content Creation and Updates:***
  - *Content Production: $30,000 to $100,000;*
  - *Multimedia Updates: $10,000 to $30,000.*
- ***Technology and Development:***
  - *App Maintenance: $15,000 to $40,000;*
  - *Continuous Technology Improvements: $20,000 to $50,000.*
- ***Marketing and User Acquisition:***
  - *Digital Marketing: $20,000 to $80,000;*
  - *User Acquisition Campaigns: $15,000 to $50,000.*
- ***Community Engagement:***
  - *Community Moderation and Management: $10,000 to $30,000;*
  - *User Engagement Initiatives: $15,000 to $50,000.*
- ***Infrastructure and Hosting:***
  - *Cloud Services: $15,000 to $40,000;*
  - *Server Maintenance: $10,000 to $30,000.*
- ***Legal and Compliance:***
  - *Ongoing Legal and Compliance Costs: $10,000 to $30,000.*
- ***Employee Salaries and Benefits:***
  - *Development Team: $60,000 to $150,000;*
  - *Marketing and Community Management: $40,000 to $100,000.*
- ***Miscellaneous:***
  - *Miscellaneous Expenses: $10,000 to $30,000.*

Total Estimated Monthly Operating Expenses: $255,000 to $660,000.

These estimations are broad and subject to change based on various factors, including the scale of the project, location, and specific requirements. Conducting a detailed financial analysis and consulting with industry experts can provide more accurate figures for your specific venture.[‡‡]

[‡‡]ChatGPT responding to the prompt "estimate the costs by category for the initial investment in this product and monthly operating expenses."

Suppose after conducting a more detailed financial analysis, the strategists estimate that the actual initial investment will be one million dollars and the monthly operating costs will be $500,000. Further, it is believed that the average transaction from subscribers and advertisers would be $10. In this case, 50,000 transactions would be required to cover monthly operating expenses, and an additional 100,000 transactions would be needed to cover the initial investment. If it is projected that there will be an average of 60,000 transactions per month, it would take 10 months to cover the initial investment, and beyond that period, the project would generate $10,000 per month in profit.

Other forces will impact the ability to price. These forces include supplier costs, competitor pricing, the willingness of the customer to pay the price, and so on. The starting point should be a thorough understanding of the breakeven point for the product or service that will be offered.

After developing a research process and identifying the state of the market, the size of the target market, the breakeven point, the distribution challenges, the competitors, and the target customer's probability of adopting the product or service, the strategist is in a position to develop a marketing strategy.

Summary

In this section, we have reviewed some research techniques that will be useful for strategists to identify the target market, the market size, the competencies needed, and financial considerations. AI can be useful in developing research initiatives. Conducting a robust situation analysis provides a sound basis for the development of a solid strategy.

CHAPTER 5

Strategy

Overview

After completing the situation analysis/research phase of the MVOSSTE process, the strategist is ready to develop a strategy. The strategy describes how the company will reach its objective by using the price it will charge, the products and services it will provide, the logistics to get the products or services to the customer, and the promotion programs it will use to create value for the customers, the collaborators, and the company. AI can be used as a tool to consider different options and approaches to address this challenge while staying in alignment with the mission, vision, objective and available resources.

Strategy

Marketing is really a study of how products and services develop trade by providing value to those participating in a marketing transaction. The participants in the marketing transaction are the customer purchasing the product or service, the company providing the product or service, and the collaborators facilitating the transaction. A successful marketing strategy requires that the company, the customers, and the collaborators receive value which is provided through the product, its price, the place or means of distributing the product, and the promotion supporting the transaction.

In short, an optimal marketing strategy is using price, place, product, and promotion (the four Ps) to create the optimal value for customers, collaborators, and the company (the three Cs).

The customers, collaborators, and the company may have differing value needs from each of the four Ps.

The value a company normally seeks is usually expressed in sales volume, profits produced and customer attitudes.

The value a collaborator normally seeks is expressed in the ability to increase sales, the ability to improve profitability, and the ability to grow the business.

The value a customer normally seeks is more difficult to determine but is based on certain drivers that influence the customer to purchase.[1] The customer adoption drivers include:

- Group Influence Intensity—Peer pressure influencing the customer;
- Perishability—Length of time the product is deemed useful;
- Psychological Appeal—Status associated with the product;
- Price Sensitivity—The need for the customer to budget;
- Relative Price Influence—The influence of price when a substitute product is considered;
- Frequency of Purchase—How often a customer purchases the product;
- Search Time Intensity—Time invested in searching for the product;
- Tangible Differentiability—Tangible physical differences from similar products;
- Intangible Differentiability—Nonphysical differences in the product;
- Technical Complexity—The need to train the user.

The successful strategist will find the price, place, product, and promotion that creates value for the customer, the collaborators, and the customer.

The Venn diagram is a depiction of the competing value goals for each of the three Cs (Figure 5.1).

The smaller overlapping areas in the diagram would suggest greater stress from Michael Porter's market forces as shown in the figure (Figure 5.2).

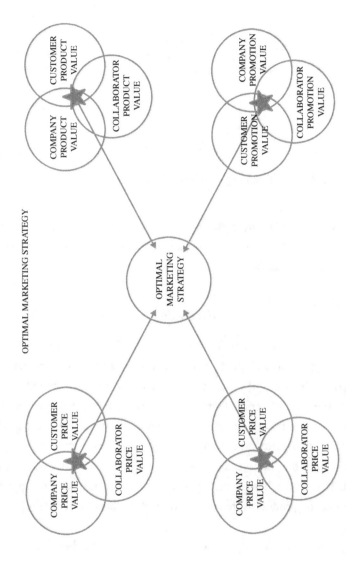

Figure 5.1 Optimal marketing strategy

Figure 5.2 Market forces affecting marketing strategy

If the overlapping areas are larger, these forces are less important. Blue Ocean and Disruptive Innovation strategies are helpful reducing the pressure of market forces.

Product

The product or service has been under consideration from the beginning of the strategic process. Starting with the mission and vision statements, setting the objective, and conducting research, the strategist should have a fix on the type of product or service to offer, the size of the target market, the competition in the marketplace, the potential sources of material, and so forth. The strategist should also have an idea of the market approach to be considered that would identify product attributes needed, the approach to launch the product (Blue Ocean, Disruptive Innovation, or product differentiation), and establish a value proposition.

A process for developing a product is depicted below (Figure 5.3).

The criteria for evaluating the product shown include:

1. Profitability/market acceptability—Will the product generate a profit and a market?
2. Accreditation requirements—Does the product meet industry and legal standards?

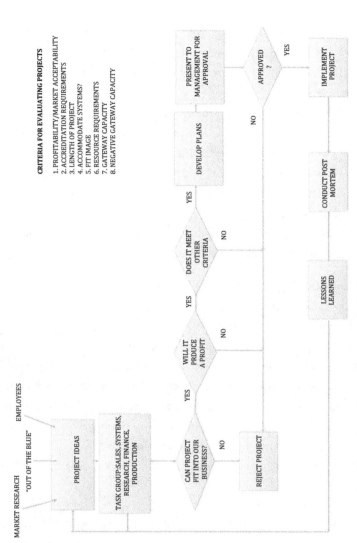

Figure 5.3 Flow chart for the product development process

3. Length of project—Can the product be introduced in an acceptable time frame?
4. Accommodate systems—Does the new product make use of current systems or will new ones need to be developed?
5. Fit Image—Does the product fit the image the firm wishes to project?
6. Resources—Is the new product resource and capital intensive?
7. Gateway capacity—Does this product lead to the possibility of new products or businesses being developed?
8. Negative gateway capacity—Does this product have the potential of damaging other products offered by the company or the company brand?
9. Customer acceptance—Will the customer accept this product over others offered in the market?

After evaluating the product idea against these criteria, developing a product strategy is in order.

For example, if a newspaper organization seeking to create a Blue Ocean strategy decided, after completing research suggested by a hypothesis tree, to launch a product focused on 18 to 30-year-old individuals who get their news from social media. The offering would be a journalism-based product that would create interest through interactivity, personalization, and the building of communities online. AI might be helpful in deciding on product attributes.

The AI-generated product strategy might provide these options for consideration:

In the first year, the newspaper aims to launch a cutting-edge social news engagement app designed to cater specifically to the preferences and habits of the 18 to 30-year-old demographic. This app will revolutionize the way news is consumed, shared, and engaged with on social media platforms.

Key Features

- **Tailored Content Streams:** *The app employs AI algorithms to curate personalized news feeds based on individual preferences, ensuring that users receive content relevant to their interests.*

- **Interactive Multimedia Stories:** *News stories are presented in dynamic formats, combining engaging visuals, videos, and interactive elements to enhance user experience and encourage social sharing.*

- **Real-Time Social Integration:** *Users can seamlessly share articles, images, and short videos directly from the app to their preferred social media platforms, facilitating organic user-generated content and expanding the news brand's reach.*

- **Collaboration With Social Media Influencers:** *The app collaborates with popular social media influencers and content creators to produce exclusive content and conduct live sessions, creating a unique blend of news and entertainment.*

- **Gamification Features:** *Introduce gamification elements to encourage user participation, such as quizzes, polls, and challenges related to news topics, fostering a sense of community engagement.*

- **Personalized Notifications:** *Utilize push notifications strategically to update users on breaking news, personalized recommendations, and exclusive content, keeping them actively engaged.*

Five-Year Product Vision: Immersive News Ecosystem

Building on the success of the one-year app, the five-year vision expands into an immersive news ecosystem that transforms the newspaper into a multifaceted media brand.

Key Features

- **Extended Content Channels:** *Diversify content channels to include podcasts, short-form documentaries, and live events, creating a comprehensive media experience beyond written articles.*

- *Virtual Reality (VR) News Experiences: Introduce VR news experiences, allowing users to virtually immerse themselves in critical events or locations, bringing an unprecedented level of immersion to news consumption.*
- *Community-Driven Journalism: Develop a community-driven journalism platform within the ecosystem, enabling users to contribute and cocreate content, fostering a sense of ownership and engagement.*
- *Blockchain-Based Authenticity: Implement blockchain technology to ensure the authenticity and transparency of news sources, addressing concerns about misinformation and fake news.*
- *Partnerships With Social Media Platforms: Forge strategic partnerships with major social media platforms for exclusive features, ensuring seamless integration and maximizing reach among the target demographic.*
- *AI-Driven Predictive Analysis: Utilize advanced AI algorithms to provide predictive analysis on emerging trends, helping users stay ahead of the curve and reinforcing the platform as a trendsetter in news delivery.*
- *Monetization Strategies: Develop innovative monetization strategies, including premium content subscriptions, virtual events, and partnerships with brands looking to connect with the young, socially active audience.*

By evolving from a social news engagement app to an immersive news ecosystem, the newspaper not only meets the evolving preferences of its 18 to 30-year-old target audience but also positions itself as a pioneering force in the media industry, embracing Blue Ocean strategies to create value for its customers, itself, and its collaborators.[*]

When deciding on the exact product components, it can be useful to do a SWOT (strengths, weaknesses, opportunities, and threats) analysis

---

[*]ChatGPT responding to the prompt "Describe the product that would meet the one and five- year objectives for a newspaper with a vision to create value for its customers, itself, and its collaborators that would use Blue Ocean strategies to attract individuals who use social media as a news source and whose target audience is 18 to 30-year-old individuals."

for each of the components to determine if they should be included. The following graphic depicts a SWOT analysis considering internal and external positive and negative effects (Figure 5.4).

AI might also be useful in generating potential names for this service. The list of names might be:

Choosing an attractive name for the social news engagement app or the immersive news ecosystem is crucial for creating a positive and memorable brand image. Here are a few name suggestions:

- *PulseSphere*
- *NewsVista*
- *InsightStream*
- *InteractiveInsider*
- *EngageHub*
- *360NewsWave*
- *TrendFlow*
- *InnoNewsHub*
- *SocialPulse Media*
- *ImmerseFeed*

When selecting a name, it's essential to consider factors such as brand identity, target audience perception, and the overall message you want to convey. Additionally, conducting a trademark search is advisable to ensure the chosen name is available and can be legally used for your product.[†]

Price

Having developed the product strategy, the pricing strategy for the product is critical. The price must be one that is accepted by the target market, is in line with potential competitors or alternative options, and must provide a profit to sustain and grow the business.

Using the example of the newspaper wishing to attract 18 to 30-year-old social media users with the product described in the product

---

[†]ChatGPT responding to the prompt "What would be an attractive name for this product?"

Figure 5.4 SWOT analysis matrix

strategy, the pricing strategy should consider all of the potential revenue sources for this product. AI can be useful in generating a list. Revenue sources could include:

A social news engagement app or an immersive news ecosystem can generate revenue through various streams. Here are potential revenue streams for this product:

- **Subscription Revenue:**
  - *Offer premium subscription plans with access to exclusive content, immersive experiences, and ad-free browsing.*
  - *Provide tiered subscription models with varying levels of features and benefits to cater to different user preferences.*
- **Ad Revenue:**
  - *Incorporate advertising within the app, generating revenue through display ads, sponsored content, and native advertising.*
  - *Offer targeted advertising options based on user preferences and behavior.*

- *In-App Purchases:*
  - Allow users to make in-app purchases for virtual goods, additional features, or premium content.
  - Offer microtransactions for specific articles, experiences, or virtual events.
- *Event Tickets and Merchandise Sales:*
  - Sell virtual event tickets for exclusive live events, Q&A sessions, or virtual reality experiences.
  - Integrate a merchandise store within the app for the sale of branded items, apparel, or other relevant products.
- *Community Contributions and Crowdfunding:*
  - Enable users to contribute to community-driven journalism through donations.
  - Launch crowdfunding campaigns for specific investigative projects or journalistic endeavors.
- *Partnerships and Sponsorships:*
  - Form partnerships with brands and sponsors for sponsored content, collaborations, and exclusive features.
  - Offer sponsorship packages for businesses looking to reach the app's target demographic.
- *Data Monetization:*
  - Analyze user behavior and preferences to provide targeted insights to advertisers and marketers.
  - Implement data-driven advertising solutions based on user analytics.
- *Educational and Corporate Plans:*
  - Provide educational plans for students, educators, or educational institutions at discounted rates.
  - Offer corporate subscriptions with tailored plans for businesses interested in staying informed.
- *Licensing and Syndication:*
  - License premium content or unique features to other media outlets, platforms, or aggregators.
  - Explore syndication agreements to expand the reach of content through third-party partnerships.
- *Virtual Reality Experiences:*

- o *Charge users for access to high-quality virtual reality news experiences or documentaries.*
- o *Collaborate with VR hardware manufacturers for revenue-sharing opportunities.*
- **Affiliate Marketing:**
  - o *Integrate affiliate marketing strategies, earning a commission for promoting products or services within the app.*
  - o *Collaborate with e-commerce platforms for affiliate partnerships related to news and information.*
- **Corporate Events and Webinars:**
  - o *Host corporate events and webinars within the app, charging businesses for participation and promotion.*
  - o *Offer sponsorship opportunities for corporate-sponsored content or events.*
- **Content Licensing and Distribution:**
  - o *License and distribute premium content to other media platforms, aggregators, or news networks.*
  - o *Explore international licensing agreements for content distribution in different regions.*
- **Dynamic Pricing and Personalized Offers:**
  - o *Implement dynamic pricing based on user behavior, preferences, and usage patterns.*
  - o *Provide personalized offers, discounts, or bundled packages to enhance user engagement.*

Diversifying revenue streams helps reduce dependency on a single source and ensures long-term sustainability. The chosen revenue model should align with the app's value proposition, user experience, and the preferences of the target demographic. Regularly assessing and adapting revenue strategies based on user feedback and market trends is essential for sustained success.[‡]

Let's assume that the strategists decide to focus on subscription revenue for the users of the app and ad revenue for businesses

---

[‡]ChatGpt responding to the prompt "What are the potential revenue streams for this product?"

wanting to reach this target market. Here the strategists should consider strategies for these models. Potential AI-generated pricing strategies might include:

For the various revenue streams mentioned earlier, different pricing models can be applied based on the nature of the product and the preferences of the target audience. Here are some pricing models for the identified revenue streams:

- **Subscription Revenue:**
  - **Flat-Rate Subscription:** *Charge users a fixed monthly or annual fee for access to all premium features.*
  - **Tiered Subscription:** *Offer different subscription tiers with increasing levels of benefits and corresponding pricing.*
- **Ad Revenue:**
  - **Cost Per Mille (CPM):** *Charge advertisers based on the number of impressions (views) their ads receive per thousand impressions.*
  - **Cost Per Click (CPC):** *Charge advertisers based on the number of clicks their ads receive.*
- **In-App Purchases:**
  - **Fixed Pricing:** *Set fixed prices for virtual goods, additional features, or premium content.*
  - **Microtransactions:** *Charge small amounts for specific in-app purchases or content pieces.*
- **Event Tickets and Merchandise Sales:**
  - **Fixed Price Tickets:** *Set a fixed price for virtual event tickets.*
  - **Variable Pricing:** *Adjust pricing based on the exclusivity or demand for specific virtual events.*
  - **Merchandise Pricing:** *Apply standard e-commerce pricing models for merchandise.*
- **Community Contributions and Crowdfunding:**
  - **Donation-Based Model:** *Allow users to contribute any amount they choose as a one-time or recurring donation.*
  - **Rewards-Based Crowdfunding:** *Offer different contribution levels with corresponding rewards or perks.*
- **Partnerships and Sponsorships:**

- o *Fixed Sponsorship Packages: Set fixed prices for different sponsorship packages with specific benefits.*
  - o *Revenue Sharing: Explore revenue-sharing agreements with sponsors based on performance metrics.*
- *Data Monetization:*
  - o *Licensing Fees: Charge businesses for access to anonymized and aggregated user data.*
  - o *Subscription-Based Data Services: Offer subscription plans for businesses seeking ongoing access to user insights.*
- *Educational and Corporate Plans:*
  - o *Discounted Flat-Rate Plans: Offer discounted flat-rate plans for students, educators, or educational institutions.*
  - o *Tiered Corporate Plans: Provide tiered plans with increasing benefits for corporate subscribers.*
- *Licensing and Syndication:*
  - o *Fixed Licensing Fees: Charge a fixed fee for the licensing of premium content.*
  - o *Royalty-Based Licensing: Negotiate a percentage-based royalty for content syndication.*
- *Virtual Reality Experiences:*
  - o *Per-Experience Pricing: Charge users for access to specific VR news experiences.*
  - o *Subscription for VR Content: Offer a separate subscription for exclusive VR content.*
- *Affiliate Marketing:*
  - o *Commission-Based Model: Earn a commission for each successful sale generated through affiliate marketing.*
  - o *Flat Fee + Commission: Combine a flat fee with a commission structure for increased revenue.*
- *Corporate Events and Webinars:*
  - o *Ticketed Events: Charge businesses a fee for participating in virtual corporate events.*
  - o *Sponsorship Packages: Offer sponsorship opportunities for corporate-sponsored events.*
- *Content Licensing and Distribution:*

- ○ **Fixed Licensing Fees:** *Charge a fixed fee for licensing premium content to other platforms.*
- ○ **Royalty-Based Licensing:** *Negotiate a percentage-based royalty for content distribution.*
- **Dynamic Pricing and Personalized Offers:**
  - ○ **Dynamic Subscription Pricing:** *Adjust subscription prices based on user behavior, preferences, and engagement levels.*
  - ○ **Personalized Offers:** *Provide customized pricing or bundled offers based on user profiles and preferences.*

Selecting the most appropriate pricing model depends on factors such as user expectations, competitive landscape, and the perceived value of the product. Combining multiple pricing models or experimenting with different approaches can help optimize revenue streams and enhance overall profitability.[§]

If the strategists thought the tiered subscription rate approach might be appropriate, the AI- generated rates and structure for a three-rate tier might look like:

The rates and content for a three-tiered subscription model can vary based on factors such as the perceived value of the content, the target audience's willingness to pay, and the features offered in each tier. Here's a hypothetical example for a social news engagement app or an immersive news ecosystem:

Basic Tier—$4.99/month

- **Access to Essential Features:**
  - ○ *Basic news articles and updates.*
  - ○ *Limited access to multimedia content.*
  - ○ *Ad-supported experience.*
  - ○ *Basic community engagement features.*

Premium Tier—$9.99/month

[§]ChatGPT responding to the prompt "What are some pricing strategies for subscription revenue and ad revenue?"

- *Enhanced Features:*
  - *Access to all basic features.*
  - *Premium articles and in-depth analysis.*
  - *Full access to multimedia content, including exclusive videos and virtual reality experiences.*
  - *Ad-free browsing experience.*
  - *Advanced community engagement features, such as forums and exclusive discussions.*

Pro or Ultimate Tier—$14.99/month

- *Comprehensive Access:*
  - *Access to all features from basic and premium tiers.*
  - *Early access to breaking news and exclusive content.*
  - *Priority access to virtual events, webinars, and live sessions.*
  - *Personalized content recommendations based on user preferences and behavior.*
  - *Premium customer support.*

Note: *These pricing figures are purely illustrative, and actual rates would depend on market research, competitive analysis, and user feedback. Additionally, offering annual subscription plans with discounted rates can encourage users to commit to long-term subscriptions.*

Additional Considerations:

- *Introductory Offers:*
  - *Offer special introductory rates or limited-time promotions to attract new subscribers.*

- *Bundle Packages:*
  - *Provide bundle packages that combine subscriptions with merchandise or virtual event tickets at a discounted rate.*
- *Student/Educational Discounts:*
  - *Consider offering discounted rates for students or educational institutions to make the app more accessible.*
- *Family Plans:*
  - *Introduce family plans allowing multiple users under a single subscription for added value.*

- **Seasonal Promotions:**
  - ○ *Implement seasonal promotions or special events with discounted rates to boost subscription numbers.*
- **Trial Periods:**
  - ○ *Provide free trial periods for the premium and pro tiers to allow users to experience the additional features before committing to a subscription.*

It's crucial to regularly reassess pricing strategies based on user engagement, market dynamics, and the evolving content landscape. Additionally, gathering feedback from subscribers can help optimize the pricing structure to better align with user expectations and maximize overall revenue.[¶]

For advertising rates, let's assume the strategists decided to focus on cost per mille (CPM) rates, cost per click (CPC) rates, and targeted advertising rates. Using AI, potential rates and structures might be:

The rates for CPM, CPC, and targeted advertising can vary widely based on factors such as the industry, target audience, ad placement, and the level of targeting specificity. Below are illustrative ranges for each pricing model:

Cost Per Mille (CPM):

- **Fixed CPM Rates:**
  - ○ **Display Ads (Standard):** *$1.50 to $5.00 CPM.*
  - ○ **Premium Display Ads (High Quality):** *$5.00 to $15.00 CPM.*
  - ○ **Video Ads:** *$10.00 to $25.00 CPM.*
  - ○ **Interactive/Immersive Ads:** *$15.00 to $40.00 CPM.*
- **Dynamic CPM Rates:**
  - ○ **Demographic Targeting:** *Additional $2.00 to $5.00 CPM for specific demographics.*
  - ○ **Behavioral Targeting:** *Additional $3.00 to $7.00 CPM based on user behavior.*

[¶]ChatGPT responding to the prompt "What would the rates and content be for a three-tiered subscription rate?"

    o **Time-Sensitive Targeting:** *Additional $1.50 to $4.00 CPM for prime time or specific time slots.*

Cost Per Click (CPC):

- **Fixed CPC Rates:**
  - o **Standard CPC:** *$0.20 to $1.00 per click.*
  - o **Premium CPC (High-Quality Audience):** *$1.00 to $5.00 per click.*
  - o **Video Ad CPC:** *$0.30 to $2.50 per click.*
- **Bid-Based CPC:**
  - o **Standard Bids:** *$0.10 to $0.50 per click.*
  - o **Competitive Bids (High Demand):** *$0.50 to $2.00 per click.*

Targeted Advertising:

- **Demographic Targeting:**
  - o **Basic Demographic Targeting:** *$2,000 to $5,000 per campaign.*
  - o **Advanced Demographic Targeting (Age, Gender, Location):** *$5,000 to $15,000 per campaign.*
- **Behavioral Targeting:**
  - o **Standard Behavioral Targeting:** *$3,000 to $8,000 per campaign.*
  - o **Custom Behavioral Segmentation:** *$8,000 to $20,000 per campaign.*
- **Contextual Targeting:**
  - o **Content-Relevant Ads:** *$2,000 to $7,000 per campaign.*
  - o **Category-Specific Contextual Targeting:** *$5,000 to $15,000 per campaign.*

Additional Considerations:

- **Ad Package Deals:**
  - o *Offer package deals for advertisers bundling CPM, CPC, and targeted advertising options at discounted rates.*
- **Performance Bonuses:**

- o   *Provide performance-based bonuses for advertisers exceeding specified engagement or conversion metrics.*
- **Seasonal Promotions:**
  - o   *Introduce special rates or discounts for advertisers during peak seasons or relevant events.*
- **Exclusive Sponsorship Opportunities:**
  - o   *Offer exclusive sponsorship opportunities with custom pricing based on the level of exclusivity and benefits provided.*
- **Dynamic Ad Pricing:**
  - o   *Implement dynamic pricing strategies based on real-time bidding or programmatic advertising for increased flexibility.*
- **Ad Formats:**
  - o   *Adjust rates based on the format of the ad, with higher rates for premium formats such as interactive or immersive ads.*

These are broad estimates, and actual rates will depend on factors specific to your app, such as audience demographics, content quality, and the competitiveness of your advertising space. Regularly assess and adjust rates based on market trends, advertiser satisfaction, and the overall performance of your ad inventory.[**]

Let's assume that research indicates the potential target market for subscribers is one million individuals and there are 150,000 potential advertisers

Using the newspaper wishing to attract 18 to 30-year-old social media users with the product described in the product strategy, financial models used in the breakeven analysis indicated that the initial investment would be one million dollars and the monthly operating costs would be $500,000 per month.

Based on the break-even analysis, the project would have to attract 50,000 customers or advertisers per month with each spending $10. This would equal about 4.3 percent of the available market.

This analysis would suggest that the subscribers would buy near the mid range of subscription rates and that advertisers would spend at the

---

[**]ChatGPT responding to the prompt "What would the rates for CPM, CPC, and targeted advertising be?"

lower end of the ad rates ($2.50 for 4,000 viewers or $1.50 for 6.66 clicks for 1000 advertisers).

Place

Place strategy refers to how a company delivers the product or service to the customer at the right place at the right time.

With the advent of the Internet and the ability to purchase items online, the marketplace has changed dramatically from the time individuals acquired products only from brick-and-mortar locations or through the mail or other delivery services. Ordering products is more convenient online than through catalogs or over the telephone.

For the marketing strategists, it is important to understand where and how their customers like to acquire their products. This can be accomplished through surveys that measure customer attitudes and purchasing habits.

The nature of the product can also have an impact on the means of distribution to the customer. Some purchases lend themselves to online purchases (online apps, books, specific mechanical parts, etc.) while others do not (automobiles, high fashion, etc.).

Customer experience also plays a large role in how a customer acquires a product and how a company distributes the product. Regardless of the mode of distribution, if the way in which a customer acquires a product is frustrating or difficult, the customer may not purchase the product. If a physical location is located where a customer has difficulty getting to the store, the customers may choose to avoid the store.

If the physical layout of the store makes it difficult for a customer to find a product, then customers may get frustrated and decide not to frequent the store again.

For online distribution, the website should be intuitive and easy to use. The websites that create obstacles or are confusing will quickly lose the ability to attract and retain customers.

AI can be useful in identifying the best methods for the distribution of a product. Here are some examples.

New Organization

For the nail clipper company used in earlier examples, the various means of distribution might be:

*A **nail clipper company** can explore various distribution channels to reach its customers. Here are some options:*

1. ***Supermarkets and Hypermarkets**: These large retail stores have a wide customer base and can help distribute nail clippers to a broad audience.*
2. ***Convenience Stores**: Conveniently located in neighborhoods, these stores cater to immediate needs and can be a good channel for nail clipper sales.*
3. ***Online Retail**: E-commerce platforms provide a global reach. Selling nail clippers online allows customers to purchase conveniently from their homes.*
4. ***Others**: This category may include specialty stores, beauty salons, or even direct sales to consumers.*

Remember that the choice of distribution channels depends on factors like target market, product positioning, and business strategy. Each channel has its advantages and challenges, so a combination of channels might be the most effective approach for a nail clipper company.[††]

For a physical location, AI can be helpful in identifying features that would appeal to potential customers. Store features might include:

*When designing a store to appeal to **nail clipper purchasers**, consider the following attributes:*

1. ***Clean and Organized Display**: A clutter-free and well-organized display allows customers to easily find nail clippers. Clear signage and proper categorization enhance the shopping experience.*
2. ***Visibility and Accessibility**: Place nail clippers in a prominent location within the store. High-traffic areas near the checkout counter or grooming section work well.*

[††]Microsoft Copilot responding to the prompt "What are some distribution channels for a nail clipper company?"

3. **Variety and Quality**: *Offer a range of nail clippers, including different sizes (for fingers and toes), materials (stainless steel, carbon steel, etc.), and designs (standard, ergonomic, or decorative). Ensure they are of good quality to build trust with customers.*

4. **Hygiene and Sanitation**: *Highlight hygiene practices. Clean, sterilized nail clippers in sealed packaging reassure buyers. Consider providing disposable testers for customers to try.*

5. **Pricing and Value**: *Transparent pricing is essential. Display price tags clearly. If offering premium nail clippers, emphasize their value (e.g., durability, precision).*

6. **Comfortable Seating**: *If the store provides nail clipping services, comfortable seating with good lighting encourages customers to try out the nail clippers.*

7. **Educational Materials**: *Informative posters or brochures about nail care, proper clipping techniques, and maintenance can engage customers and promote sales.*

8. **Customer Service**: *Friendly and knowledgeable staff who can guide customers in choosing the right nail clippers enhance the overall experience.*

9. **Eco-Friendly Options**: *Consider offering eco-friendly nail clippers made from sustainable materials. Environmentally conscious consumers appreciate such choices.*

10. **Promotions and Bundles**: *Seasonal discounts, buy-one-get-one offers, or nail clipper sets (with files, cuticle pushers, etc.) attract attention.*

Remember, creating a positive shopping environment and addressing customer needs will make your store appealing to nail clipper purchasers.[‡‡]

Design of the website for online purchasers requires consideration of the customers' online purchasing requirements. Again, AI can be helpful here. Some features for a website selling nail clippers might include:

[‡‡]Microsoft Copilot responding to the prompt "What attributes should a store have to appeal to nail clipper purchasers?"

When designing a website to attract **online purchasers of nail clippers**, consider incorporating the following features to enhance user experience and drive sales:

1. **Clear Product Descriptions**: Provide detailed information about each nail clipper, including material (e.g., stainless steel), size, and edge shape (e.g., curved). Clarity helps customers make informed decisions.[1]

2. **High-Quality Images**: Showcase nail clippers from various angles. High-resolution images allow users to examine details and build confidence in their purchase.

3. **User Reviews and Ratings**: Display authentic reviews and ratings from previous buyers. Positive feedback builds trust and encourages potential customers to proceed with their purchase.

4. **Easy Navigation**: Ensure a user-friendly interface with clear menus and categories. Customers should find nail clippers effortlessly.

5. **Responsive Design**: Optimize the website for mobile devices. Many users shop on their phones, so a mobile-friendly site is crucial.

6. **Search Functionality**: Implement a search bar to help users find specific nail clippers quickly.

7. **Secure Checkout Process**: Assure customers that their payment information is safe. Use SSL (protocol that encrypts communications in apps) certificates and display trust badges.

8. **Product Filters**: Allow users to filter nail clippers by attributes such as price, material, or type (e.g., fingernail or toenail clippers).

9. **Related Products**: Suggest complementary items, such as nail files or cuticle pushers, to encourage additional purchases.

10. **Promotions and Discounts**: Highlight any ongoing sales, bundle deals, or limited-time offers.

11. **Contact Information**: Provide clear contact details, including customer support, e-mail, or chat, for inquiries or assistance.

12. **Shipping and Return Policies**: Clearly state shipping costs, delivery times, and return procedures. Transparency builds trust.

13. **Live Chat Support**: Offer real-time assistance to address customer queries promptly.

14. *Social Proof: Showcase social media links or integrate Instagram feeds displaying user-generated content related to nail clippers.*

Remember, a well-designed website that prioritizes user experience and addresses customer needs will attract online purchasers of nail clippers![§§]

Existing Company

Using the example of a newspaper wishing to reach 18 to 30-year-old social media users, AI-generated suggested channels of distribution might include:

*If a newspaper company aims to attract **18 to 30-year-old social media users**, it should strategically utilize channels that resonate with this demographic. Here are some effective distribution channels:*

1. *Instagram: With **72** percent of this age group using Instagram, it's an ideal platform for visual content distribution. The company can share engaging news snippets, behind-the-scenes stories, and captivating visuals.*
2. *TikTok: As **35** percent of 18 to 29-year-olds are on TikTok, the newspaper can create short, informative videos or even participate in trending challenges to reach this audience.*
3. *YouTube: YouTube boasts **85** percent usage among this demographic. The newspaper can produce video content, including interviews, explainers, and feature stories, to engage young viewers.*
4. *Snapchat: With **41** percent of 18 to 29-year-olds active on Snapchat, the company can leverage its stories feature to share bite-sized news updates and exclusive content.*
5. *X formerly **Twitter**: Although **32** percent of this age group uses Twitter, it's still a valuable channel for real-time news updates, discussions, and engaging with readers.*

Remember, the key is to tailor content to each platform's unique strengths and engage with the audience authentically.[§§]

[§§]Microsoft Copilot responding to the prompt "What features should a website have to attract online purchasers of nail clippers?"

AI generated features of a website for the newspaper wishing to reach 18 to 30-year-old social media users might include:

*When designing a website to attract **18 to 30-year-old social media users**, consider incorporating the following features to enhance user experience and engagement:*

1. ***Mobile-First Design****: Optimize your website for mobile devices. Young users predominantly access content via smartphones, so a responsive design is crucial.*

2. ***Fast Loading Times****: Millennials and Gen Z expect instant gratification. Ensure your website loads quickly to retain their attention.*

3. ***Social Media Integration***
   o ***Share Buttons****: Include social sharing buttons for articles. Users can easily share interesting content with their networks.*
   o ***Embedded Feeds****: Display real-time social media feeds (e.g., Twitter or Instagram) related to news topics.*

4. ***Personalization***
   o ***Customized Content****: Use algorithms to recommend articles based on users' interests and browsing history.*
   o ***User Profiles****: Allow users to create profiles, save favorite articles, and receive personalized newsletters.*

5. ***Visual Appeal***
   o ***High-Quality Images****: Use captivating visuals to accompany articles.*
   o ***Video Content****: Incorporate video news segments or interviews.*

6. ***Interactive Elements***
   o ***Polls and Quizzes****: Engage users with interactive polls or quizzes related to news topics.*
   o ***Comments and Discussions****: Enable users to comment on articles and participate in discussions.*

7. ***Easy Navigation***

---

[55]Microsoft Copilot responding to the prompt " What are some channels of distribution for content from a newspaper company wishing to attract 18 to 30-year-old social media users?"

- ○ **Clear Menus**: *Organize content into intuitive categories (e.g., News, Lifestyle, Opinion).*
- ○ **Search Bar**: *Allow users to search for specific topics or articles.*
8. **Breaking News Alerts**
    - ○ **Push Notifications**: *Notify users instantly about breaking news or important updates.*
9. **Community Building**
    - ○ **User-Generated Content**: *Encourage users to submit their stories, photos, or opinions.*
    - ○ **Events and Meetups**: *Promote local events related to news or community gatherings.*
10. **Social Proof**
    - ○ **Showcase User Reviews**: *Highlight positive feedback from other readers.*
    - ○ **Display Social Media Followers**: *Demonstrate your newspaper's popularity on social platforms.*

Remember, understanding your target audience's preferences and habits is essential for creating a website that resonates with young social media users!"***

In all of the AI generated suggestions, the strategist should recognize that these are options and should be adjusted to fit the capabilities and needs of the organization.

Promotion

The final part of the strategy that has to be carefully developed is promotion.

The Job to Be Done

Promotion is the communication that describes the job the product or service will do for the target market. The obvious use might not be the use desired by the customer. For example, the purchase of an

---

***Microsoft Copilot responding to the prompt "What features should a website have for a newspaper to attract 18 to 30-year-old social media users?"

automobile might be as much to satisfy the status needs of the customer as providing a mode of transportation.

AI can be helpful in understanding the potential "jobs" a product can do. For the newspaper wishing to attract 18 to 30-year-old social media users, the jobs that might be considered for their offering might be:

If a newspaper is launching a new product to cater to 18 to 30-year-old social media users, the offerings would likely need to align with the preferences, interests, and behaviors of this demographic. Here are potential jobs or functions that such a product could perform to engage and attract this audience:

- ***Bite-Sized News Updates:***
  - *Delivering concise and easily digestible news updates tailored to the interests of young adults.*
- ***Interactive Content:***
  - *Providing interactive content such as polls, quizzes, and surveys to engage users in a participatory manner.*
- ***Video News:***
  - *Creating short, engaging video content to deliver news stories in a visually appealing format.*
- ***Live News Coverage:***
  - *Offering live streaming of important events or breaking news for real-time engagement.*
- ***Personalized News Feeds:***
  - *Implementing algorithms to curate personalized news feeds based on users' preferences and behavior.*
- ***In-depth Features:***
  - *Including in-depth features and long-form articles on topics relevant to the interests of the 18 to 30 age group.*
- ***Entertainment News:***
  - *Incorporating entertainment news, celebrity updates, and pop culture content to appeal to younger audiences.*
- ***Social Media Integration:***
  - *Seamless integration with popular social media platforms to allow for easy sharing and discussion.*

- **User-Generated Content:**
  - Encouraging users to contribute content, share their opinions, and participate in community discussions.
- **Community Building:**
  - Fostering a sense of community through forums, discussion boards, or social media groups.
- **Interactive Storytelling:**
  - Using interactive storytelling techniques to make news narratives more engaging.
- **Customizable News Alerts:**
  - Allowing users to customize news alerts and notifications based on their preferences.
- **Visual Storytelling:**
  - Incorporating visually appealing graphics, infographics, and multimedia elements to enhance storytelling.
- **Mobile-Friendly Design:**
  - Ensuring a responsive and mobile-friendly design for on-the-go access.
- **Localized News:**
  - Providing hyperlocalized news content relevant to the specific interests and concerns of local communities.
- **Podcasts:**
  - Offering news podcasts or audio content for users who prefer to consume information through audio formats.
- **Social Responsibility Features:**
  - Highlighting social and environmental issues, as younger audiences often value socially responsible content.
- **Events and Experiences:**
  - Hosting virtual or in-person events, webinars, or experiences related to news topics and trends.
- **Integration With Emerging Platforms:**
  - Exploring integration with emerging platforms and technologies that resonate with the tech-savvy younger demographic.
- **Educational Content:**
  - Providing educational content on important issues, trends, or skills that matter to young adults.

The key is to create a product that not only delivers news but also aligns with the lifestyle, preferences, and digital habits of the 18 to 30-year-old demographic. By offering a mix of informative, entertaining, and community-driven features, the product can become a valuable source of information and engagement for this age group.[†††]

Identify Media for Each Customer Segment

Customers for any product will come from different demographic and psychographic groups. Segmenting the potential customer base and identifying media is necessary to effectively deliver the messages needed to move the market to action. AI can be helpful in identifying media to be used in a campaign. For the newspaper wishing to attract 18 to 30-year-old social media users, the AI-generated media list would be different and look like:

To effectively promote a new web-based product offered by a newspaper company to 18 to 30-year-old social media users, it's crucial to use channels that resonate with this demographic. Here are media options tailored for this audience:

- ***Social Media Platforms:***
  - *Leverage popular platforms such as Instagram, Facebook, Twitter, and Snapchat to reach the younger audience. Create engaging content, including visuals, videos, and stories.*
- ***Influencer Marketing:***
  - *Collaborate with influencers or social media personalities within the 18 to 30 age range. Influencers can create authentic content, reviews, and tutorials about the new web-based product.*
- ***YouTube Advertising:***
  - *Run targeted video ads on YouTube, focusing on content relevant to the interests of the younger demographic. Consider working with YouTubers who align with the product's theme.*

[†††]ChatGPT responding to the prompt "What are the jobs that would be performed by a new product offered by a newspaper to reach 18 to 30-year-old social media users?"

- *TikTok Campaigns:*
  - Utilize TikTok, a platform popular among younger users, for creative and short-form video campaigns. Encourage user-generated content related to the web-based product.
- *Social Media Contests:*
  - Run contests and giveaways on social media platforms to generate excitement and encourage user participation. This can help increase awareness and engagement.
- *Social Media Advertising:*
  - Invest in targeted social media advertising to reach specific demographics. Utilize features like Instagram and Facebook ads to tailor campaigns to the interests of 18 to 30-year-olds.
- *E-mail Marketing:*
  - Build an e-mail marketing strategy to communicate directly with the target audience. Send newsletters with updates, promotions, and exclusive content related to the web-based product.
- *Podcast Sponsorships:*
  - Sponsor podcasts that are popular among the 18 to 30 age group. Podcast advertising can be an effective way to reach a captive audience.
- *Digital Billboards:*
  - Use digital billboards in urban areas and popular locations frequented by the target demographic. Incorporate visually appealing and dynamic content.
- *Online Streaming Services:*
  - Consider advertising on platforms like Spotify, Pandora, or other music streaming services that are popular among younger audiences.
- *Interactive Content:*
  - Develop interactive content such as quizzes, polls, and challenges on social media to engage users and create a sense of interactivity.
- *Social Media Influencers Takeovers:*

> ○ *Allow social media influencers to take over the newspaper's social media accounts for a day to showcase the web-based product and connect with their audience.*

- **Community Engagement:**
  - ○ *Participate in online communities and forums where the target audience is active. Engage in discussions and share information about the new web-based product.*

- **Geotargeted Campaigns:**
  - ○ *Implement geotargeting in advertising campaigns to reach users in specific locations where the 18 to 30 age group is concentrated.*

- **Branded Hashtags:**
  - ○ *Create and promote branded hashtags across social media platforms to encourage user-generated content and build a community around the new product.*

- **Interactive Advertising Formats:**
  - ○ *Utilize interactive ad formats on social media platforms to capture attention and encourage users to explore the features of the web-based product.*

- **Mobile App Advertising:**
  - ○ *Advertise within mobile apps that are popular among the target demographic. Consider in-app ads that align with the interests of 18 to 30-year-olds.*

- **Social Media Live Sessions:**
  - ○ *Conduct live sessions on platforms like Instagram or Facebook to introduce and demonstrate the features of the web-based product in real time.*

Tailoring the media strategy to the preferences and behaviors of the 18 to 30 age group is essential for successful promotion. Regularly monitor analytics and user engagement to refine the approach and ensure effective communication.[‡‡‡]

[‡‡‡]ChatGPT responding to the prompt "What media should be used by a newspaper company to promote its new web-based product to 18 to 30-year-old social media users?"

Moving an Audience to Act

It is important to understand that a potential customer has to go through several phases of an adoption process to move a potential customer to purchase the product. According to Roger Wimmer, the steps in that process that would be the focus of promotion campaigns are:

- Unaware—The point at which the potential customer doesn't realize the product exists.
- Aware—Making potential customers aware that the product or service exists.
- Comprehension—The point at which potential customers understand what the product does.
- Conviction—The point at which potential customers are convinced the product would fit their needs.
- Action—The point at which customers are moved to purchase the product (Figure 5.5).

All promotion campaigns should be aware that there are some potential customers that are at each stage of the knowledge continuum. AI can be helpful in developing messages for each of the knowledge phases. For example, AI-generated taglines for the newspaper focused on the 18 to 30-year-old social media users might be:

Here are taglines for each phase of the newspaper company's advertising campaign targeting 18 to 30-year-old social media users:

- ***Unaware Phase:***
  - *Tagline: "Ignite Your Feed with Fresh Perspectives."*
  - *Message: "Unaware of the buzz? Brace yourself for a new wave of content that speaks directly to your interests. Ignite your feed with us."*
- ***Aware Phase:***
  - *Tagline: "Stay Connected, Stay Informed—[Newspaper Name] Knows."*

UNAWARE → AWARE → COMPREHENSION → CONVICTION → ACTION

Figure 5.5 Steps to move customers to make purchase decisions

- o   *Message: "Now that you're aware, stay connected and stay informed with [Newspaper Name]. Dive into content that resonates with your world."*
- **Comprehension Phase:**
  - o   *Tagline: "Beyond the Headlines, Dive into the Stories that Matter."*
  - o   *Message: "Comprehend the depth of our content. Beyond the headlines, discover stories that matter and perspectives that resonate."*
- **Conviction Phase:**
  - o   *Tagline: "Empower Your Narrative, Choose [Newspaper Name]."*
  - o   *Message: "You're convinced—empower your narrative with [Newspaper Name]. Join a community that values your voice and your stories."*
- **Action Phase:**
  - o   *Tagline: "Swipe, Read, Share—Your Daily Connection Starts Now."*
  - o   *Message: "Ready to take action? Swipe through, read, and share. Your daily connection to meaningful content starts now with [Newspaper Name]."*

These taglines aim to engage 18 to 30-year-old social media users through different stages, emphasizing the newspaper's unique value proposition and encouraging them to take action in their daily media consumption habits.[§§§]

[§§§]ChatGPT responding to the prompt "What are some messages and taglines that can be used for customers at each stack of the adoption process (unaware, aware, comprehension, conviction, and action) for a newspaper wishing to attract 18 to 30-year-old social media users?"

Determining the Budget

Determining the budget can be difficult in that it requires balancing the financial resources available, the messages to the market segments through the various media, and the impact needed to move the customer through the knowledge phases.

Using the example of the newspaper earlier wishing to attract 18 to 30-year-old media users and having a promotion budget of $130,000 per month, an AI-generated media budget might look like:

Let's allocate the budget across different media channels to guide potential customers through the knowledge phases (unaware, aware, comprehension, conviction, Action) for a monthly budget of $130,000 and a goal of achieving 600,000 transactions per month:

- *Unaware Phase (20% of Budget):*
  - *Tagline: "Ignite Your Feed with Fresh Perspectives."*
  - *Message: "Unaware of the buzz? Brace yourself for a new wave of content that speaks directly to your interests. Ignite your feed with us."*
- *Allocation: $26,000*
  - *Social Media Advertising: $15,000*
  - *Influencer Marketing: $11,000*
- *Aware Phase (20% of Budget):*
  - *Tagline: "Stay Connected, Stay Informed—[Newspaper Name] Knows."*
  - *Message: "Now that you're aware, stay connected and stay informed with [Newspaper Name]. Dive into content that resonates with your world."*
- *Allocation: $26,000*
  - *Social Media Advertising: $10,000*
  - *YouTube Advertising: $6000*
  - *Influencer Marketing: $10,000*
- *Comprehension Phase (15% of Budget):*
  - *Tagline: "Beyond the Headlines, Dive into the Stories that Matter."*

- o   Message: *"Comprehend the depth of our content. Beyond the headlines, discover stories that matter and perspectives that resonate."*
- **Allocation:** *$19,500*
  - o   *Sponsored Content and Branded Challenges: $9,000*
  - o   *Social Media Contests and Giveaways: $5,500*
  - o   *Influencer Marketing: $5,000*
- **Conviction Phase (15% of Budget):**
  - o   *Tagline: "Empower Your Narrative, Choose [Newspaper Name]."*
  - o   *Message: "You're convinced—empower your narrative with [Newspaper Name]. Join a community that values your voice and your stories."*
- **Allocation:** *$19,500*
  - o   *Influencer Marketing: $8,000*
  - o   *Podcast Sponsorships: $7000*
  - o   *Social Media Live Sessions: $4,500*
- **Action Phase (30% of Budget):**
  - o   *Tagline: "Swipe, Read, Share—Your Daily Connection Starts Now."*
  - o   *Message: "Ready to take action? Swipe through, read, and share. Your daily connection to meaningful content starts now with [Newspaper Name]."*
- **Allocation:** *$39,000*
  - o   *Digital Billboards: $7,000*
  - o   *Branded Hashtags and Challenges: $8,000*
  - o   *Social Media Live Sessions: $6,000*
  - o   *Geotargeted Campaigns: $10,000*
  - o   *Interactive Advertising: $8,000*

Total Monthly Budget: $130,000

This budget distribution is designed to strategically move potential customers through the awareness journey, ensuring each phase is adequately addressed with the right mix of media channels and messaging. Adjustments can be made based on performance analytics and ongoing optimization efforts.￼￼￼

Aligning With the Brand

The brand is critical to the success of a company, and the company's products, messages, and actions should be in alignment with the company's mission. The brand speaks to both internal and external audiences. The brand conveys what the company promises and its core values.

Thus, all actions taken by the company, its media messages, and its operating procedures should be in alignment with the brand and its mission and vision statements.

Summary

A marketing strategy incorporates product, price, place, and promotion to create value for the customer, the company, and its collaborators. It is important to keep this in mind while setting the strategy for each of the four Ps. Generative AI can be a helpful tool when developing the overall marketing strategy and giving the strategist a sense of all the options that can be considered.

Having developed a research-based strategy allows the organization to consider approaches that may be used to deploy the strategy.

¶¶¶ChatGPT responding to the prompt "Assuming a monthly budget of $130,000 promotion and customer acquisition and using the taglines and media above for the newspaper focused on 18 to 30-year-old social media users, create a media budget that will be 600,000 transactions per month. Divide the allocations by media to move the potential customers through the knowledge phases: unaware, aware, comprehension, conviction, action."

CHAPTER 6

Tactics

Overview

Creating a strategy has provided the basis for achieving the objectives established. Tactics identify the resources and processes that will be needed to carry out the strategy. AI can assist in identifying approaches to acquiring needed resources and developing processes.

Tactics

Tactics are the actions and resources that will need to be taken to deploy the strategy. This involves the workforce, financial requirements, operating procedures, and capital equipment required for strategy deployment.

A good way of thinking about developing the tactics is to consider how they interact with the price, place, product, and promotion (the 4Ps) of the strategy.

In the grid below, each of the 4Ps are aligned with each tactical element: workforce, cash requirements, operating procedures and fixed assets.

This allows the strategist to consider tactics that fit with the strategy to create value for the customers, collaborators and the company.

If research has provided a good guide to profitability with specific cost limits, it may be necessary to consider several options to achieve the best outcome.

Workforce

The workforce composition might be comprised of full and part time employees, contractors, use of vendors for some activities related to the products or services they provide and in some cases volunteers. This mix of workforce sources can be utilized to maximize product value, control costs, and ensure value creation goals are met.

Workforce compensation can also play a significant role in the ability to successfully deploy a strategy. The compensation can involve salaried, commission, or hourly positions. Certain jobs can be paid using a piece rate or payment based on production. For key positions stock options or ownership can be offered.

Another component of the workforce to be considered is logistics. The workforce can have individuals working remotely or onsite. The cost of the chosen logistics mix is important. To have an effective workforce, the organization may need to assume the cost of equipment for remote workers or the cost of transportation for some positions requiring travel.

Newspaper Example

AI can be helpful in developing a structure to consider workforce options. For example, in the case of a newspaper wishing to attract 18 to 30-year-old social media users with a payroll of $300,000 (based on the breakeven worksheet and financial analysis), a workforce plan might look like:

Workforce Plan for [Newspaper Name]—$300,000 Payroll Budget

Workforce Composition

- **Salaried Positions (30% of Budget—$90,000):**
    o *Editorial Team: Journalists, Editors, Content Curators*
    o *Marketing Team: Social Media Strategists, Brand Managers*
    o *Technology Team: Developers, UX/UI Designers*
- **Hourly Positions (20% of Budget—$60,000):**
    o *Social Media Moderators*

PLANNING THE STRATEGY

COPYRIGHT GWR RESEARCH	OPTIMAL PRICE	OPTIMAL PLACE	OPTIMAL PRODUCT	OPTIMAL PROMOTION
WORKFORCE (EMPLOYEES, CONTRACTORS ALLIANCES, PARTNERS	WORKFORCE COSTS ARE WITHIN ACCEPTABLE LEVELS TO PRODUCE NEEDED PROFIT WITH PROJECTED OPTIMAL PRICING AND SALES	WORKFORCE IS AVAILABLE FOR OPERATION AT OPTIMAL LOCATION AND SUPPORTS SUPPLY CHAIN EFFICIENCY	WORKFORCE CAN EFFICIENTLY PRODUCE OPTIMAL PRODUCT WITHIN ACCEPTABLE QUALITY REQUIREMENTS	WORKFORCE CAN PRODUCE AND DELIVER OPTIMAL PROMOTION AND SALES CAMPAIGNS WITH HIGH DEGREE OF EFFICACY
CASH REQUIREMENTS	REVENUES GENERATED WITH OPTIMAL PRICING PROVIDES SUFFICIENT CASH FLOW TO MEET OPERATIONAL AND GROWTH NEEDS	OPTIMAL LOCATION AND LOGISTICS ENHANCE CASH FLOWS AND MINIMIZE CASH OUTLAYS	OPTIMAL PRODUCT OPTIMIZES OPERATING MARGINS, INVENTORY TURNS AND CASH FLOWS	OPTIMAL PROMOTION OPTIMIZES MIX OF MEDIA TO EFFICIENTLY BUILD CUSTOMER BASE AND MOVE CUSTOMERS TO ACTION
OPERATING PROCEDURES	OPTIMAL PRICE IS MANAGED BY BY SETTING PROPER SALES GOALS, DISCOUNTS AND ESTABLISHING METRICS TO MONITOR CONTRIBUTION MARGIN PER UNIT	OPTIMAL PLACE IS MANAGED BY ESTABLISHING METRICS (INVENTORY COST/SQ.FT., PROFIT/SQ.FT.)	OPTIMAL PRODUCT IS MANAGED BY ESTABLISHING METRICS (R&D COSTS/SALES, MATERIAL WASTE PER UNIT, PAYROLL/UNIT)	OPTIMAL PROMOTION IS MANAGED BY CREATING METRICS FOR PROMOTION COSTS (AD COST/REVENUE, NEW CUSTOMER ACQUISITION COST ETC.)
FIXED ASSETS	OPTIMAL PRICE SUPPORTS REQUIRED FIXED ASSETS (LEASE VS. BUY)	OPTIMAL PLACE MAXIMIZES PRODUCTIVITY OF REQUIRED ASSETS (QUANTITY AND PLACEMENT OF ASSETS)	OPTIMAL PRODUCT MAXIMIZES PRODUCTIVITY OF ASSETS	OPTIMAL PROMOTION MAXIMIZES PRODUCTIVITY OF REQUIRED ASSTES

- o   *Customer Support Representatives*
- *Contract Positions (15% of Budget—$45,000):*
  - o   *Influencers and Content Creators*
  - o   *Graphic Designers for Campaigns*
- *Piecemeal Rates (10% of Budget—$30,000):*
  - o   *Freelance Writers and Contributors*
  - o   *Photographers and Videographers for Events*
- *Full-Time Positions (10% of Budget—$30,000):*
  - o   *Editorial Team Leads*
  - o   *Marketing Team Leads*
  - o   *Technology Team Leads*
- *Part-Time Positions (5% of Budget—$15,000):*
  - o   *Social Media Moderators*
  - o   *Customer Support Representatives*
- *Commission-Based Positions (5% of Budget—$15,000):*
  - o   *Sales Representatives for Premium Subscriptions*
  - o   *Ad Sales Representatives for Sponsored Content*
- *Use of Vendors (5% of Budget—$15,000):*
  - o   *Collaborate With Social Media Management Platforms*
  - o   *Outsource Printing and Distribution for Physical Promotional Materials*

Workforce Strategy

- *Recruitment and Onboarding (10% of Budget—$30,000):*
  - o   *Utilize cost-effective recruitment channels, such as social media and online platforms.*
  - o   *Conduct virtual onboarding sessions to minimize costs associated with physical presence.*
- *Training and Skill Development (10% of Budget—$30,000):*
  - o   *Leverage online training platforms for skill development programs.*
  - o   *Implement a mentorship program to enhance skills within the team.*
- *Flexibility and Remote Work (5% of Budget—$15,000):*

- o   *Offer flexible work hours to accommodate hourly and part-time positions.*
- o   *Implement remote work policies, reducing overhead costs.*
- **Performance Incentives (5% of Budget—$15,000):**
  - o   *Introduce performance-based incentives for commission-based roles.*
  - o   *Recognize outstanding contributions through cost-effective reward programs.*

Workforce Engagement

- **Internal Communication (5% of Budget—$15,000):**
  - o   *Utilize affordable communication tools for internal collaboration.*
  - o   *Implement regular virtual team-building activities.*
- **Feedback Mechanism (3% of Budget—$9,000):**
  - o   *Establish a streamlined feedback system using cost-effective online platforms.*
  - o   *Conduct regular virtual feedback sessions to gather insights.*
- **Wellness Programs (2% of Budget—$6,000):**
  - o   *Introduce cost-effective wellness initiatives, such as virtual fitness classes.*
  - o   *Promote mental health awareness through online resources.*
- **Career Growth Opportunities (5% of Budget—$15,000):**
  - o   *Provide low-cost online courses and certifications for professional development.*
  - o   *Implement a mentorship program to foster career growth.*

Workforce Sustainability

- **Succession Planning (3% of Budget—$9,000):**
  - o   *Develop an internal talent pool through mentorship programs.*
  - o   *Plan for smooth transitions in key roles to minimize disruptions.*
- **Adaptability to Industry Changes (5% of Budget—$15,000):**
  - o   *Encourage a culture of continuous learning and adaptability.*
  - o   *Invest in affordable resources to stay updated on industry trends.*

- ***Employee Retention Strategies (5% of Budget—$15,000):***
  - ○ *Implement cost-effective retention strategies, such as recognition programs.*
  - ○ *Regularly assess and address factors influencing employee satisfaction.*
- ***Community Engagement (2% of Budget—$6,000):***
  - ○ *Engage with the target audience through low-cost social media initiatives.*
  - ○ *Gather user feedback to enhance workforce planning strategies.*

This workforce plan is designed to align with a $300,000 payroll budget, ensuring a cost-effective approach to attract, engage, and retain a diverse workforce focused on capturing the attention of 18 to 30-year-old social media users. Adjustments can be made based on performance analytics and ongoing optimization efforts.[*]

The strategist can eliminate or add to the positions and the related costs. Any cost adjustments would require an update to breakeven analyses.

The workforce can be refined by asking AI to consider how the workforce is impacted by the 4Ps and might look like:

Workforce Plan for [Newspaper Name]

Workforce Composition:

- ***Customer Support Team (40% of Budget—$120,000):***
  - ○ *Hire dedicated customer support representatives to handle interactions through various channels.*
  - ○ *Include a mix of full-time and part-time roles to ensure coverage during peak hours.*
- ***Social Media Moderation Team (25% of Budget—$75,000):***

---

[*]ChatGPT responding to the prompt "Considering workforce composition of salaried, hourly, contract, piecemeal rates, full time, part time, commission and use of vendors, create a workforce plan for the newspaper wishing to attract 18 to 30-year-old social media users and limited to a $300,000 payroll budget."

- o *Assemble a team responsible for moderating and engaging on social media platforms.*
- o *Consider part-time roles to cover evenings and weekends when social media activity is high.*
- **Content Creation and Editorial Team (20% of Budget— $60,000):**
  - o *Employ content creators, writers, and editors to produce engaging content tailored to the 18 to 30 age group.*
  - o *Emphasize creativity and a deep understanding of social media trends.*
- **Marketing and Promotion Team (15% of Budget—$45,000):**
  - o *Build a team focused on promoting the newspaper's content through various channels.*
  - o *Invest in digital marketing experts, influencers, and creative designers.*

Workforce Strategy

- **Customer Support:**
  - o *Implement a tiered support system with basic queries handled by entry-level representatives and complex issues escalated to experienced team members.*
  - o *Utilize chatbots and AI tools for routine inquiries to improve efficiency.*
- **Social Media Moderation:**
  - o *Train the team on social media trends, community guidelines, and crisis management.*
  - o *Encourage active engagement with the audience to foster a sense of community.*
- **Content Creation and Editorial:**
  - o *Foster a creative environment, allowing team members to pitch and execute innovative content ideas.*
  - o *Implement an editorial calendar to ensure consistent and timely content publication.*
- **Marketing and Promotion:**

- o *Develop targeted marketing campaigns focusing on social media platforms popular among the target audience.*
- o *Collaborate with influencers and leverage user-generated content for organic promotion.*

Logistics Favorable for Workforce

- **Remote Work Opportunities:**
  - o *Enable remote work options, especially for roles like social media moderation and content creation.*
  - o *Use collaboration tools to ensure effective communication among remote team members.*
- **Flexible Scheduling:**
  - o *Implement flexible scheduling, allowing part-time employees to work during peak social media activity hours.*
  - o *Ensure coverage during evenings and weekends when engagement is high.*
- **Cross-Training:**
  - o *Cross-train team members to handle multiple responsibilities, enhancing flexibility during peak periods.*

Ability to Promote the Service

- **Influencer Collaborations:**
  - o *Leverage influencers from the 18 to 30 age group to promote the newspaper.*
  - o *Encourage influencers to share their experiences and engage with their followers.*
- **Interactive Campaigns:**
  - o *Run interactive campaigns and challenges to involve the audience.*
  - o *Utilize social media platforms to amplify the reach of promotional activities.*
- **User-Generated Content:**
  - o *Encourage users to create and share content related to the newspaper.*

○ *Feature user-generated content in marketing materials for authenticity.*

Performance Metrics and Optimization

- ***Customer Interaction Monitoring:***
  ○ *Implement tools to monitor and analyze customer interactions, ensuring prompt and effective responses.*
  ○ *Use key performance indicators (KPIs) to measure customer satisfaction.*
- ***Social Media Analytics:***
  ○ *Monitor social media analytics to assess the impact of promotions and engagement campaigns.*
  ○ *Adjust strategies based on real-time performance data.*
- ***Content Engagement Metrics:***
  ○ *Track content engagement metrics such as views, likes, and shares.*
  ○ *Optimize content strategies based on audience preferences.*

This workforce plan, considering a $300,000 monthly payroll budget, aims to efficiently manage customer interactions, promote the service, and create a dynamic and adaptable workforce aligned with the goal of attracting and engaging 18 to 30-year-old social media users. Adjustments can be made based on performance analytics and ongoing optimization efforts.[†]

Having considered the structure and composition of the workforce, it will be important to tie the workforce structure to the price, place, product, and promotion components of the overall marketing strategy. AI can be helpful in developing a tactical structure.

Building an effective workforce is crucial for the success of a newspaper targeting 18 to 30-year-old social media users. Here's a set of tactics addressing workforce considerations for price, place, product, and promotion within the

---

[†]ChatGPT resending to the prompt "Considering a newspaper wising to attract 18 to 30-year-old social media users with a $300,000 monthly payroll budget, create a workforce plan that considers the volume of 60,000 customer interactions per month, the logistics favorable for the workforce and the ability to promote the service."

given monthly expense budget of $500,000 to achieve 60,000 transactions per month:

Price Tactics

- ***Pricing Analyst:***
  - ○ ***Tactic:*** *Hire a pricing analyst to optimize subscription plans and dynamic pricing strategies.*
  - ○ ***Workforce Requirement:*** *Allocate budget for a pricing analyst who can analyze market trends, user behavior, and competition to optimize pricing for subscriptions and promotions.*
- ***Customer Support Representatives:***
  - ○ ***Tactic:*** *Employ a customer support team to handle pricing-related inquiries.*
  - ○ ***Workforce Requirement:*** *Allocate budget for customer support representatives who can assist users with pricing queries, subscription management, and dispute resolution.*

Place Tactics

- ***Digital Platform Developers:***
  - ○ ***Tactic:*** *Employ developers to enhance digital platforms and ensure cross-platform integration.*
  - ○ ***Workforce Requirement:*** *Allocate budget for a development team that can maintain, update, and optimize the newspaper's website and mobile applications.*
- ***IT Support Staff:***
  - ○ ***Tactic:*** *Hire IT support staff to ensure smooth operation of technology infrastructure.*
  - ○ ***Workforce Requirement:*** *Allocate budget for IT professionals who can handle technical issues, server maintenance, and cybersecurity.*
- ***Content Management Specialists:***
  - ○ ***Tactic:*** *Employ content management specialists to streamline content creation processes.*

    o **Workforce Requirement:** *Allocate budget for specialists who can manage the content creation workflow, ensuring timely and relevant articles.*

Product Tactics

- **Editorial Team:**
  - o **Tactic:** *Build a skilled editorial team for high-quality content production.*
  - o **Workforce Requirement:** *Allocate budget for editors, writers, and multimedia content creators who can produce engaging and relevant content.*
- **User-Generated Content Moderators:**
  - o **Tactic:** *Hire moderators to oversee user-generated content.*
  - o **Workforce Requirement:** *Allocate budget for content moderators who can ensure a safe and positive user experience in interactive features.*
- **Agile Development Team:**
  - o **Tactic:** *Establish an agile development team for iterative product improvements.*
  - o **Workforce Requirement:** *Allocate budget for developers and project managers who can implement user feedback and continuously enhance product features.*

Promotion Tactics

- **Marketing Team:**
  - o **Tactic:** *Build a marketing team for data-driven promotional campaigns.*
  - o **Workforce Requirement:** *Allocate budget for marketing professionals who can analyze user data, plan targeted campaigns, and execute promotions effectively.*
- **Social Media Managers:**
  - o **Tactic:** *Employ social media managers for consistent brand messaging.*

○ **Workforce Requirement:** *Allocate budget for social media professionals who can manage the newspaper's presence on various platforms, engage with the audience, and implement social media strategies.*

- **Content Creation Team:**
  ○ **Tactic:** *Establish a team for creating visually appealing promotional content.*
  ○ **Workforce Requirement:** *Allocate budget for graphic designers, video editors, and multimedia specialists who can create compelling promotional materials.*

Overall Workforce Considerations

- **Training and Development:**
  ○ *Allocate budget for ongoing training programs to keep the workforce updated on industry trends, technologies, and best practices.*
- **Flexible Talent Acquisition:**
  ○ *Consider a mix of full-time, part-time, and contract positions to optimize workforce flexibility within budget constraints.*
- **Performance Metrics and Incentives:**
  ○ *Implement performance metrics and incentive programs to motivate the workforce and align their efforts with organizational goals.*
- **Regular Workforce Reviews:**
  ○ *Regularly review workforce effectiveness, making adjustments as needed based on performance metrics and user feedback.*

By strategically allocating budget towards the workforce, the newspaper can build a talented and adaptable team that supports the goal of generating 60,000 transactions per month among the target audience. Regular workforce assessments and adjustments will contribute to sustained success.[‡]

[‡]ChatGPT responding to the prompt "For a newspaper with a monthly expense budget of $500,000, trying to reach 18 to 30-year-old social media users, develop a set of tactics for the cash requirements needed to have a successful organization generating 60,000 transactions per month. Address cash requirements as they relate to price, place, product, and promotion."

Cash Requirements

Cash requirements refer to the use of cash needed to operate the organization in a manner that will achieve its goals. Cash requirement tactics should address both cash inflows and outflows. By tying the cash requirement to the price, place, product, and promotion components of strategy, the tactics will have a more complete view of the activities and uses of cash.

Generative AI can quickly provide an outline that the strategist can use when developing a cash budget.

Newspaper Example

An AI-generated cash plan for the newspaper trying to attract 18 to 30-year-old social media users might look like:

Developing tactics for a newspaper targeting 18 to 30-year-old social media users with a monthly expense budget of $500,000 and aiming for 60,000 transactions per month requires careful consideration of price, place, product, and promotion. Here's a set of tactics addressing cash requirements for each element:

Price Tactics

- **Freemium Model:**
    - o **Tactic:** *Offer basic access to news content for free.*
    - o **Cash Consideration:** *Allocate budget for maintaining and updating free content, focusing on high-quality articles and engaging multimedia.*
- **Tiered Subscription Pricing:**
    - o **Tactic:** *Introduce tiered subscription plans with varying levels of benefits.*
    - o **Cash Consideration:** *Allocate budget for creating premium content, exclusive features, and ad-free experiences. Consider introductory pricing to attract early subscribers.*

- *Discounts and Promotions:*
  - o *Tactic:* Run limited-time promotions or student discounts.
  - o *Cash Consideration:* Allocate budget for promotional campaigns and ensure that discounted plans are financially sustainable in the short term.

Place Tactics

- *Digital Platforms Optimization:*
  - o *Tactic:* Optimize the newspaper's presence on popular digital platforms.
  - o *Cash Consideration:* Invest in digital marketing strategies to enhance visibility, including paid social media ads and search engine optimization.
- *Cross-Platform Accessibility:*
  - o *Tactic:* Ensure the newspaper is accessible across various devices.
  - o *Cash Consideration:* Allocate budget for responsive web design, mobile app development, and compatibility testing.
- *Collaboration With Social Media Platforms:*
  - o *Tactic:* Explore partnerships with social media platforms for increased reach.
  - o *Cash Consideration:* Invest in sponsored content, partnerships, and promotions on social media platforms.

Product Tactics

- *User-Centric Content Development:*
  - o *Tactic:* Develop content that resonates with the target audience.
  - o *Cash Consideration:* Allocate budget for hiring skilled writers, photographers, and multimedia content creators. Invest in audience research for content ideation.
- *Innovative Features and Interactivity:*
  - o *Tactic:* Introduce interactive features like polls, quizzes, and user-generated content.
  - o *Cash Consideration:* Invest in technology development for interactive features. Allocate budget for maintaining and moderating user-generated content.

- **Regular Product Iterations:**
  - o **Tactic:** *Continuously iterate the product based on user feedback.*
  - o **Cash Consideration:** *Allocate a portion of the budget for regular updates, improvements, and incorporating user suggestions.*

Promotion Tactics

- **Influencer Collaborations:**
  - o **Tactic:** *Partner with influencers to promote the newspaper.*
  - o **Cash Consideration:** *Allocate budget for influencer marketing, considering influencers with high engagement among the target demographic.*
- **Targeted Advertising:**
  - o **Tactic:** *Run targeted digital advertising campaigns.*
  - o **Cash Consideration:** *Allocate budget for paid social media advertising, ensuring ads are well-targeted to reach the intended audience.*
- **Community Engagement:**
  - o **Tactic:** *Foster community engagement through social media.*
  - o **Cash Consideration:** *Allocate budget for social media management, community building initiatives, and user engagement campaigns.*

Overall Considerations

- **Performance Analytics:**
  - o *Implement robust analytics to measure the performance of various tactics.*
  - o *Allocate budget for analytics tools and data analysis.*
- **Agile Budgeting:**
  - o *Maintain flexibility in budget allocation based on the performance of different tactics.*
  - o *Regularly review and adjust the budget to optimize spending.*
- **User Acquisition Costs:**
  - o *Keep a close eye on user acquisition costs.*

    o *Allocate budget efficiently to acquire new users while maintaining a reasonable cost per acquisition.*

By strategically allocating the budget across price, place, product, and promotion tactics, the newspaper can effectively reach its target audience, generate transactions, and create a sustainable business model within the given expense constraints. Regularly assessing performance metrics will enable ongoing optimization and adaptation to market dynamics.[§]

Operating Procedures

Operating procedures refer to the processes and methods that will be employed to ensure that the strategy is implemented successfully. By tying the development of the operating procedures to the price, place, product, and promotion components of the marketing strategy, the strategist is including all key strategic components.

Again, generative AI can be helpful in outlining a tactical plan.

Newspaper Example

Using the newspaper example from above, the AI-generated operating procedures might look like:

Operating procedures play a crucial role in the success of a newspaper targeting 18 to 30-year-old social media users. Here's a set of tactics addressing operational aspects for price, place, product, and promotion within the given monthly expense budget of $500,000 to achieve 60,000 transactions per month:

Price Tactics

• ***Dynamic Pricing Model:***

[§]ChatGPT responding to the prompt "For a newspaper with a monthly expense budget of $500,000, trying to reach 18 to 30-year-old social media users, develop a set of tactics for the operating procedures needed to have a successful organization generating 60,000 transactions per month. Address cash requirements as they relate to price, place, product, and promotion."

- o **Tactic:** *Implement a dynamic pricing model that adapts based on user engagement and demand.*
- o **Operational Consideration:** *Regularly analyze user behavior and adjust pricing tiers to optimize revenue. Utilize analytics tools to monitor user interactions.*

- **Automated Subscription Management:**
  - o **Tactic:** *Implement an automated subscription management system.*
  - o **Operational Consideration:** *Reduce manual workload in managing subscriptions. Allocate budget for subscription management software to streamline operations.*

- **Promotion Budget Optimization:**
  - o **Tactic:** *Allocate a portion of the budget specifically for promotions and discounts.*
  - o **Operational Consideration:** *Regularly review the performance of promotions and adjust the budget allocation based on the effectiveness of different campaigns.*

Place Tactics

- **Cross-Platform Integration:**
  - o **Tactic:** *Integrate the newspaper's presence seamlessly across digital platforms.*
  - o **Operational Consideration:** *Invest in cross-platform integration tools to ensure consistency in content delivery. Monitor platform-specific metrics to optimize engagement.*

- **Content Delivery Optimization:**
  - o **Tactic:** *Optimize content delivery for a smooth user experience.*
  - o **Operational Consideration:** *Regularly assess website and app performance. Allocate budget for content delivery network (CDN) services to enhance speed and reliability.*

- **Real-Time Customer Support:**
  - o **Tactic:** *Implement real-time customer support through chatbots and online help desks.*

o ***Operational Consideration:*** *Train support staff for efficient handling of user inquiries. Use automation tools to streamline responses.*

Product Tactics

- ***Agile Content Production:***
  - o ***Tactic:*** *Adopt an agile content production approach for timely and relevant articles.*
  - o ***Operational Consideration:*** *Foster collaboration between editorial and technology teams. Allocate budget for project management tools to enhance workflow efficiency.*
- ***User-Generated Content Moderation:***
  - o ***Tactic:*** *Encourage user-generated content while moderating for quality and relevance.*
  - o ***Operational Consideration:*** *Implement automated content moderation tools to ensure a safe and engaging environment. Allocate budget for human moderators as needed.*
- ***Iterative Development:***
  - o ***Tactic:*** *Continuously iterate product features based on user feedback.*
  - o ***Operational Consideration:*** *Implement agile development methodologies. Allocate budget for regular software updates and improvements.*

Promotion Tactics

- ***Data-Driven Marketing:***
  - o ***Tactic:*** *Utilize data analytics for targeted and personalized promotions.*
  - o ***Operational Consideration:*** *Invest in analytics tools for user segmentation and behavior analysis. Allocate budget for marketing automation software.*
- ***Social Media Management:***
  - o ***Tactic:*** *Streamline social media management for consistent brand messaging.*

- o ***Operational Consideration:*** *Utilize social media manage-ment tools. Allocate budget for sponsored posts and advertising.*
- **Content Calendar Planning:**
  - o ***Tactic:*** *Plan content calendars aligned with promotional activities.*
  - o ***Operational Consideration:*** *Use editorial calendars and project management tools to coordinate content creation and promotion schedules.*

Overall Operational Considerations

- **Expense Tracking and Reporting:**
  - o *Regularly track expenses and generate reports to monitor budget allocation.*
  - o *Allocate budget for financial management tools.*
- **Team Training and Development:**
  - o *Invest in continuous training for teams, ensuring they are equipped with the latest skills and knowledge.*
  - o *Allocate budget for training programs and workshops.*
- **Risk Management:**
  - o *Establish a risk management plan to mitigate unforeseen challenges.*
  - o *Allocate a contingency budget for unexpected operational issues.*
- **Regular Review and Adaptation:**
  - o *Conduct regular reviews of operational processes and adapt based on performance metrics.*
  - o *Allocate budget for process optimization tools and consultancy if needed.*

By implementing these operational tactics, the newspaper can efficiently manage its resources within the budget constraints while striving for the goal of 60,000 transactions per month among the target audience. Regular monitoring and adaptation to operational strategies are crucial for sustained success.¶

¶ChatGPT responding to the prompt "For a newspaper with a monthly expense budget of $500,000, trying to reach 18 to 30-year-old social media users, develop a set of tactics for the fixed assets needed to have a successful organiza-

Fixed Assets

Fixed assets are fixtures and equipment required to conduct business operations. When considering fixed assets, besides considering price, place, product, and promotion strategies, the method of acquisition should also be considered.

Using generative AI to develop a tactical structure for fixed assets might look like:

Fixed assets are essential for the long-term success and sustainability of a newspaper targeting 18 to 30-year-old social media users. Here's a set of tactics addressing fixed assets for price, place, product, and promotion within the given monthly expense budget of $500,000 to achieve 60,000 transactions per month:

Price Tactics

- ***Subscription Management Software:***
  - ○ ***Tactic:*** *Invest in a robust subscription management system.*
  - ○ ***Fixed Asset Requirement:*** *Allocate a portion of the budget for purchasing or subscribing to subscription management software, ensuring efficient handling of subscription plans, billing, and customer management.*
- ***Pricing Optimization Tools:***
  - ○ ***Tactic:*** *Utilize tools for dynamic pricing optimization.*
  - ○ ***Fixed Asset Requirement:*** *Allocate budget for pricing optimization software that can adapt pricing strategies based on user behavior, market trends, and promotional activities.*
- ***Payment Gateway Integration:***
  - ○ ***Tactic:*** *Ensure seamless and secure payment processing.*
  - ○ ***Fixed Asset Requirement:*** *Invest in integrating a reliable payment gateway into the newspaper's digital platforms, providing users with multiple payment options.*

---

tion generating 60,000 transactions per month. Address cash requirements as they relate to price, place, product, and promotion."

Place Tactics

- **Content Delivery Network (CDN):**
  - ○ *Tactic: Enhance website and app performance with a CDN.*
  - ○ *Fixed Asset Requirement: Allocate budget for subscribing to a reputable CDN service to improve content delivery speed and reliability.*
- **Cross-Platform Integration Tools:**
  - ○ *Tactic: Optimize the newspaper's presence across various digital platforms.*
  - ○ *Fixed Asset Requirement: Invest in tools and software that facilitate cross-platform integration, ensuring a consistent user experience across devices.*
- **Technology Infrastructure:**
  - ○ *Tactic: Invest in robust technology infrastructure.*
  - ○ *Fixed Asset Requirement: Allocate budget for servers, storage, and other essential hardware to support the newspaper's digital operations.*

Product Tactics

- **Content Management System (CMS):**
  - ○ *Tactic: Implement a user-friendly CMS for efficient content creation and management.*
  - ○ *Fixed Asset Requirement: Allocate budget for purchasing or customizing a CMS that meets the specific needs of the newspaper.*
- **Interactive Features Development Tools:**
  - ○ *Tactic: Enhance user engagement with interactive features.*
  - ○ *Fixed Asset Requirement: Invest in development tools and software that facilitate the creation of interactive elements within the content.*
- **User-Generated Content Moderation Tools:**
  - ○ *Tactic: Encourage user-generated content while maintaining quality.*
  - ○ *Fixed Asset Requirement: Implement automated content moderation tools to ensure a safe and engaging environment.*

Promotion Tactics

- ***Marketing Automation Software:***
  - ○ ***Tactic:*** *Implement marketing automation for targeted campaigns.*
  - ○ ***Fixed Asset Requirement:*** *Allocate budget for marketing automation software that streamlines promotional activities and improves efficiency.*
- ***Social Media Management Tools:***
  - ○ ***Tactic:*** *Streamline social media management for consistent brand messaging.*
  - ○ ***Fixed Asset Requirement:*** *Invest in social media management tools to schedule posts, track engagement, and analyze performance.*
- ***Content Creation and Editing Software:***
  - ○ ***Tactic:*** *Ensure high-quality visual content for promotional materials.*
  - ○ ***Fixed Asset Requirement:*** *Allocate budget for graphic design and video editing software to create visually appealing promotional content.*

Overall Fixed Asset Considerations

- ***Technology Upgrades and Maintenance:***
  - ○ *Regularly allocate a portion of the budget for technology upgrades and maintenance to ensure fixed assets remain up-to-date and efficient.*
- ***Asset Life Cycle Management:***
  - ○ *Implement an asset life cycle management strategy to maximize the usefulness of fixed assets over time.*
- ***Security Infrastructure:***
  - ○ *Allocate budget for cybersecurity measures to protect fixed assets from potential threats.*

By strategically allocating budget toward these fixed assets, the newspaper can ensure a strong foundation for its operations, supporting the goal of generating 60,000 transactions per month among the target audience.

Regular reviews and updates to fixed assets are essential for staying competitive and meeting evolving user expectations.[**]

Summary

Understanding the 4Ps of marketing strategy is crucial to laying out the tactics for each of the 4Ps. Using the MVOSSTE approach requires the strategist to first identify the critical marketing strategy components and then develop a tactical plan for each component.

Generative AI can be helpful in identifying tactical components and relating them to the price, place, product, and promotion components of the overall marketing strategy. The MVOSSTE approach helps identify prompts for AI that will lead to a more complete tactical plan.

The tactics identify the resources and processes needed to deploy the strategy and set the stage for the execution phase of the MVOSSTE process.

[**]ChatGPT resending to the prompt "For a newspaper with a monthly expense budget of $500,000, trying to reach 18 to 30-year-old social media users, develop a set of tactics for the workforce needed to have a successful organization generating 60,000 transactions per month. Address cash requirements as they relate to price, place, product, and promotion."

CHAPTER 7

Execution

Overview

This chapter will discuss the actions required to implement the tactics identified in the previous chapter.

Execution

Using the MVOSSTE approach, the final stage of developing a complete marketing plan is execution. Using research, the strategist has developed a solid marketing strategy built around price, place, product, and promotion. Using the key components of the strategy, the strategist then identified the tactics that would best be used when deploying the strategy.

The next stage of the MVOSSTE approach is developing the plan to act on the tactics that will successfully deploy the strategy. This is the execution stage and consists of four components that are directly related to the tactical components. For each tactical component of the workforce, cash requirements, operating procedures, and fixed assets, the strategist must have an overall plan, an organizational plan, a plan for directing the resources, and a means of measuring and controlling the plans to ensure success.

In the following grid, the relationship between the tactical components and the execution components is shown. For each tactical component of the workforce, cash requirements, operating procedures, and fixed assets, there must be an overall plan, an organizational plan, a means of directing actions, and a means of controlling or monitoring outcomes.

Again, generative AI can be helpful in developing each component of the execution phase.

IMPLEMENTING THE STRATEGY

COPYRIGHT GWR RESEARCH	STRATEGIC WORKFORCE	STRATEGIC CASH REQUIREMENTS	STRATEGIC OPERATING PROCEDURES	STRATEGIC FIXED ASSETS
PLANNING	DEVELOP JOB DESCRIPTIONS AND STANDARDS OF PERFORMANCE TO REACH OPTIMUM STRATEGY	DEVELOP ACCOUNTS RECEIVABLE AND PAYABLE PROCEDURES TO ENHANCE CASH FLOWS	DEVELOP OPERATING PROCEDURES THAT ENSURE BEST QUALITY CONTROL AND VALUE DELIVERY	DEVELOP PROCESS FOR IDENTIFYING OPTIMAL FIXED ASSETS ACQUISITION AND DEPLOYMENT (LEASE VS. BUY)
ORGANIZING	WORKFORCE SHOULD B ORGANIZED IN A MANNER THAT EFFICIENTLY SUPPORTS OPTIMUM STRATEGY	ESTABLISH FINANCIAL MECHANISMS TO MAXIMIZE EFFICIENT USE OF CASH	OPERATING GROUPS AND DEPARTMENTS SHOULD BE ORGANIZED TO OPTIMIZE STRATEGIC RESULTS	ASSETS ORGANIZED TO SUPPORT ORGANIZATIONAL PRODUCTIVITY
DIRECTING	STANDARDS OF PERFORMANCE TIED TO NEEDED OUTCOMES TO ACIEVE OPTIMAL STRATEGY (EG, PRODUCTS/HR.)	CASH FLOW DIRECTED TO HIGHEST AND BEST USE IN THE ORGANIZATION (PROMOTION VS, EXPANSION VS. ACQUISITION)	OPERATING PROCESSES SUPPORT OPTIMUM STRATEGIC GOALS (SUPPLY CHAIN, SALES COMMISSION STRUCTURE)	ASSETS DEPLOYED TO SUPPORT STRATEGIC GOALS (EQUIPMENT AVAILABLE WHEN NEEDED)
CONTROLLING	METRICS FOR PAY AND BONUSES ARE TIED TO STANDARDS OF PERFORMANCE	METRICS DESIGNED AND MANAGED TO ASSURE EFFICIENT CASH USEAGE'	METRICS ARE DESIGNED TO MAXIMIZE OPERATIONAL EFFICIENCY AND EFFECTIVENESS	METRICS ARE DESIGNED TO MAXIMIZE ASSET PRODUCTIVITY

Before an action can be taken, it is wise to develop a plan to ensure all actions are in line with the objectives that they are supporting the strategy and in line with the organization's mission and vision.

Since the tactical components were tied to the marketing strategy components that were based on research and supported the mission and vision of the organization, the plan should carefully consider each tactical component.

The first step is to develop a program to plan, organize, direct, and control for each tactical component:

- The workforce—Organization, needed positions, responsibilities, and standards of performance for each position.
- Cash needs and uses—Cash flow design, how money will be collected, used, and invested.
- Operating procedures—Methods, key performance indicators, and other metrics that will be needed and used to track success.
- Fixed assets—How assets will be acquired (lease or purchase) and how they will be utilized.

Workforce

Planning

For this exercise, we will continue to use AI to assist in the creation of the plans. The reader is encouraged to view the footnotes that describe the prompts used to direct AI and the previous grid to see how the prompts were developed.

An AI-generated workforce plan might look like:and areas for improvement, e

Here are the key positions, their responsibilities, and standards of performance for a newspaper targeting 18 to 30-year-old social media users with a monthly expense budget of $500,000, aiming to generate 60,000 transactions per month:

Pricing Analyst

- ***Responsibilities:***

- o   *Analyze market trends, user behavior, and competition to optimize subscription plans and dynamic pricing strategies.*
- o   *Monitor and adjust pricing tiers based on performance metrics and promotional activities.*
- o   *Provide insights on pricing structures to maximize revenue and user acquisition.*
- **Standards of Performance:**
  - o   *Achieve a set target for optimizing pricing strategies and increasing subscription revenue.*
  - o   *Regularly analyze and report on the effectiveness of pricing tactics.*
  - o   *Respond promptly to pricing-related inquiries and implement adjustments as needed.*

Customer Support Representatives

- **Responsibilities:**
  - o   *Assist users with pricing queries, subscription management, and dispute resolution.*
  - o   *Provide timely and helpful responses to customer inquiries via various channels (e-mail, chat, social media).*
  - o   *Collaborate with other teams to address customer concerns and improve overall user experience.*
- **Standards of Performance:**
  - o   *Meet or exceed customer satisfaction targets.*
  - o   *Respond to customer inquiries within defined time frames.*
  - o   *Collaborate with the pricing analyst to gather feedback on user concerns related to pricing.*

Digital Platform Developers

- **Responsibilities:**
  - o   *Enhance and maintain the newspaper's website and mobile applications for optimal user experience.*
  - o   *Ensure cross-platform integration for seamless content delivery.*

o *Collaborate with IT support to address technical issues and improve platform performance.*
- *Standards of Performance:*
  - o *Ensure high website and app performance metrics (speed, reliability, responsiveness).*
  - o *Implement updates and improvements based on user feedback and industry best practices.*
  - o *Minimize downtime and address technical issues promptly.*

IT Support Staff

- *Responsibilities:*
  - o *Handle technical issues related to servers, infrastructure, and cybersecurity.*
  - o *Ensure the security and reliability of technology assets.*
  - o *Collaborate with developers to implement technology upgrades and maintenance.*
- *Standards of Performance:*
  - o *Maintain a secure technology infrastructure with minimal downtime.*
  - o *Respond promptly to technical issues and implement solutions.*
  - o *Collaborate with developers to ensure seamless integration of technology assets.*

Editorial Team

- *Responsibilities:*
  - o *Produce high-quality and engaging content targeted at the 18 to 30-year-old demographic.*
  - o *Ensure timely publication of relevant articles, multimedia content, and interactive features.*
  - o *Collaborate with the pricing and marketing teams to align content with promotional activities.*
- *Standards of Performance:*
  - o *Meet content production targets, ensuring a regular and varied content schedule.*

- o *Monitor user engagement metrics for content and iterate based on feedback.*
- o *Align content strategy with the overall goals of the organization.*

Marketing Team

- **Responsibilities:**
  - o *Plan and execute data-driven promotional campaigns to acquire and retain users.*
  - o *Analyze user data and market trends to inform marketing strategies.*
  - o *Collaborate with the editorial team to align content with promotional activities.*
- **Standards of Performance:**
  - o *Achieve user acquisition and retention targets.*
  - o *Monitor the effectiveness of marketing campaigns through key performance indicators (KPIs).*
  - o *Collaborate with the pricing and editorial teams to ensure a cohesive marketing strategy.*

Social Media Managers

- **Responsibilities:**
  - o *Manage the newspaper's presence on various social media platforms.*
  - o *Engage with the audience through regular posts, interactions, and community building.*
  - o *Implement social media strategies to increase brand visibility and user engagement.*
- **Standards of Performance:**
  - o *Increase social media followers and engagement metrics.*
  - o *Monitor and respond to social media trends, adapting strategies accordingly.*
  - o *Collaborate with the marketing team to integrate social media into overall promotional campaigns.*

Content Moderation Team

- **Responsibilities:**
  - *Oversee user-generated content to ensure a safe and positive user experience.*
  - *Implement content moderation policies and guidelines.*
  - *Collaborate with the editorial team to highlight user-generated content in a positive manner.*
- **Standards of Performance:**
  - *Maintain a positive and engaging community environment.*
  - *Respond promptly to user-reported content issues.*
  - *Collaborate with the editorial team to feature high-quality user-generated content.*

These positions, responsibilities, and standards of performance form a cohesive workforce strategy for the newspaper, ensuring alignment with the overall goal of generating 60,000 transactions per month among the target audience. Regular reviews and adjustments based on performance metrics will contribute to sustained success. [*]

It is important to understand an AI-generated program will require analysis and will change based on the unique needs of an organization. No matter how carefully a prompt is developed to generate an AI response, it may not precisely meet the needs of an organization. In this case, the organization may want to have fewer people, spend less money, or put more emphasis on a certain area. AI can be used to refine the effort but may require adjustments that meet the precise needs of the organization.

Organizing

Having the workforce organized in an efficient manner is important to achieving organizational goals. It is important to understand the link between the organizational functions and the role each plays in the organization's success.

---

[*]ChatGPT responding to the prompt "For a newspaper with a monthly expense budget of $500,000, trying to reach 18 to 30-year-old social media users, using the set of tactics for the workforce needed to have a successful organization generating 60,000 transactions per month. Identify the positions needed with responsibilities and standards of performance for each position."

AI can be helpful here as well but as the strategist develops the execution elements, the prompts for AI will need to be more detailed in describing what is needed.

Here is an AI-generated response to a request for an organizational structure for the newspaper in question (note the specificity of the prompt in the footnote following the AI response).

To effectively support the goals of reaching 18 to 30-year-old social media users and generating 60,000 transactions per month, the newspaper requires a well-defined organizational structure encompassing all operational functions. Below is a proposed organization structure:

Executive Leadership

- ***Chief Executive Officer (CEO):***
  - *Oversees the overall strategic direction and performance of the newspaper.*
  - *Sets goals, objectives, and KPIs for the organization.*
- ***Chief Operating Officer (COO):***
  - *Manages day-to-day operations and ensures efficient workflow across departments.*
  - *Coordinates with department heads to implement strategic initiatives.*

Editorial Department

- ***Editor-in-Chief:***
  - *Leads the editorial team in creating high-quality and engaging content.*
  - *Sets editorial policies and guidelines.*
- ***Content Editors:***
  - *Responsible for content planning, creation, and publication.*
  - *Manage a team of writers, reporters, and content creators.*
- ***Multimedia Team:***
  - *Produces visual and multimedia content, including videos, graphics, and interactive features.*

Digital Operations

- **Digital Platform Manager:**
  - Oversees the development and maintenance of the newspaper's digital platforms.
  - Ensures user-friendly design, functionality, and performance.
- **IT Support Team:**
  - Provides technical support and ensures the security and reliability of digital infrastructure.

Marketing and Promotion

- **Chief Marketing Officer (CMO):**
  - Develops and implements marketing strategies to acquire and retain users.
  - Manages advertising campaigns and promotional activities.
- **Social Media Managers:**
  - Manages the newspaper's presence on social media platforms.
  - Engages with the audience and implements social media strategies.
- **Content Marketing Team:**
  - Creates and distributes promotional content to attract and engage users.

Sales and Revenue Generation

- **Chief Revenue Officer (CRO):**
  - Leads revenue generation efforts and oversees sales operations.
  - Develops partnerships and advertising opportunities.
- **Advertising Sales Team:**
  - Identifies and secures advertising opportunities from advertisers.
  - Negotiates ad placements and sponsorship deals.

Customer Support and Engagement

- **Customer Support Manager:**
  - Manages a team of customer support representatives.
  - Handles user inquiries, feedback, and issue resolution.

- ***Community Managers:***
  - o *Fosters community engagement and moderates user-generated content.*

Finance and Administration

- ***Chief Financial Officer (CFO):***
  - o *Manages financial planning, budgeting, and reporting.*
  - o *Ensures compliance with financial regulations.*
- ***Accounting and Billing Team:***
  - o *Handles accounts payable and receivable, billing, and invoicing.*

Human Resources

- ***Human Resources Manager:***
  - o *Oversees recruitment, onboarding, training, and performance management.*
  - o *Manages employee relations and benefits administration.*

This organization structure ensures clear roles, responsibilities, and communication channels to support the newspaper's goals of reaching the target demographic and achieving transaction targets. Collaboration between departments is essential for cohesive operations and achieving overall success.[†]

Directing

Even with a clear definition of jobs and a good organizational structure, an organization will not have optimum results unless every position works together toward achieving the organization's goals. Each position should have a defined responsibility (what must be accomplished), a standard (the definition of success in fulfilling the responsibility), and a metric that clearly measures how well the standard was met.

[†]ChatGPT responding to the prompt "For a newspaper with a monthly expense budget of $500,000, trying to reach 18 to 30-year-old social media users, using the set of tactics for the workforce needed to have a successful organization generating 60,000 transactions per month. Create an organization structure that includes all operational functions to support reaching its goals."

Below is an example of a standard of performance for a sales position. When this is provided for each position and each supports the organization's goals, there is a strong probability that the organization's goal will be met.

Standards of Performance Account Executive

Responsibility	Standard	Metric (4 = 100%)
1. Provide Daily Sales Activity	1. Daily Entry In CRM	20 Entries = 4, 15 To 19 = 2
2. 2 Cold Calls Per Week	2. Weekly Sales Report	2 Cold Calls = 4, 1 Cc=2
3. 5 Sales Per Month	3. Monthly Sales Report	5 Sales = 4, 3 Sales = 2

Using AI, this job can be made easier but will have to be reviewed carefully to ensure that the organization's goals are supported.

Here's a standard of performance for each position within the organization structure of a newspaper targeting 18 to 30-year-old social media users, aiming to generate 60,000 transactions per month with a monthly expense budget of $500,000:

Pricing Analyst

> **Responsibility:** *Analyze market trends, user behavior, and competition to optimize subscription plans and dynamic pricing strategies.*
> **Standard for Fulfillment:** *Regularly review pricing strategies and adjust subscription plans based on market analysis.*
> **Metric for Success:** *Increase in subscription revenue by X percent quarterly.*

Customer Support Representatives

> **Responsibility:** *Assist users with pricing queries, subscription management, and dispute resolution.*
> **Standard for Fulfillment:** *Respond to customer inquiries within 24 hours and resolve 80 percent of issues on the first contact.*

Metric for Success: Maintain a customer satisfaction rating of 90 percent or higher.

Digital Platform Developers

Responsibility: Enhance and maintain the newspaper's website and mobile applications for optimal user experience.

Standard for Fulfillment: Implement updates and improvements based on user feedback within two weeks of identification.

Metric for Success: Decrease in website/app loading time by X percent within six months.

IT Support Staff

Responsibility: Handle technical issues related to servers, infrastructure, and cybersecurity.

Standard for Fulfillment: Address technical issues within one hour of notification and minimize downtime to less than 1 percent per month.

Metric for Success: Maintain an uptime rate of 99.9 percent or higher.

Editorial Team

Responsibility: Produce high-quality and engaging content targeted at the 18 to 30-year-old demographic.

Standard for Fulfillment: Publish X number of articles/videos per week, covering diverse topics relevant to the target audience.

Metric for Success: Increase in user engagement metrics (page views, shares, comments) by X percent monthly.

Marketing Team:

Responsibility: Plan and execute data-driven promotional campaigns to acquire and retain users.

Standard for Fulfillment: Launch X number of marketing campaigns per quarter with clear objectives and measurable KPIs.

Metric for Success: *Increase in user acquisition rate by X percent quarterly.*

Social Media Managers

Responsibility: *Manage the newspaper's presence on various social media platforms.*

Standard for Fulfillment: *Post engaging content daily across all social media channels and respond to user comments/queries within one hour.*

Metric for Success: *Increase in social media followers and engagement metrics by X percent monthly.*

Content Moderation Team

Responsibility: *Oversee user-generated content to ensure a safe and positive user experience.*

Standard for Fulfillment: *Monitor user-generated content regularly and remove any inappropriate or offensive content within 24 hours.*

Metric for Success: *Maintain a zero-tolerance policy for harmful content and receive no more than X user complaints per month.*

By establishing clear standards of performance for each position, the newspaper can ensure alignment with organizational goals and track progress effectively toward reaching its target of 60,000 transactions per month. Regular performance evaluations and adjustments based on metrics will contribute to the organization's success.[‡]

[‡]ChatGPT responding to the prompt "For a newspaper with a monthly expense budget of $500,000, trying to reach 18 to 30-year-old social media users, using the set of tactics for the workforce needed to have a successful organization generating 60,000 transactions per month Create a standard of performance for each position that defines its responsibility, establishes a standard for fulfilling the responsibility, and provides a metric for determining the level of success."

Controlling

Having pay grades and bonuses tied to standards of performance ensures that everyone knows their job, that it supports the organization's goals, and that meeting or exceeding the standards set will result in success for the organization and the individual employees.

Having AI do the initial structure will help identify goals and pay structure.

To establish pay grades and bonuses tied to each position's standards of performance, we can use a combination of objective metrics and subjective evaluations. Here's how it can be structured:

Pricing Analyst

- ***Objective Metrics:***
    - *Increase in subscription revenue.*
- ***Pay Grade and Bonus:***
    - *Base salary + bonus tied to the percentage increase in subscription revenue achieved quarterly.*

Customer Support Representatives

- ***Objective Metrics:***
    - *Customer satisfaction rating.*
- ***Pay Grade and Bonus:***
    - *Base salary + bonus tied to maintaining or exceeding the target customer satisfaction rating.*

Digital Platform Developers

- ***Objective Metrics:***
    - *Decrease in website/app loading time, successful implementation of user feedback.*
- ***Pay Grade and Bonus:***
    - *Base salary + bonus tied to achieving the target decrease in loading time and successful implementation of user feedback.*

IT Support Staff

- **Objective Metrics:**
  - Uptime rate, response time to technical issues.
- **Pay Grade and Bonus:**
  - Base salary + bonus tied to maintaining or exceeding the target uptime rate and response time to technical issues.

Editorial Team

- **Objective Metrics:**
  - User engagement metrics (page views, shares, comments).
- **Pay Grade and Bonus:**
  - Base salary + bonus tied to increasing user engagement metrics by the target percentage.

Marketing Team

- **Objective Metrics:**
  - User acquisition rate, success of marketing campaigns.
- **Pay Grade and Bonus:**
  - Base salary + bonus tied to achieving or exceeding the target user acquisition rate and success of marketing campaigns.

Social Media Managers

- **Objective Metrics:**
  - Increase in social media followers and engagement metrics.
- **Pay Grade and Bonus:**
  - Base salary + bonus tied to achieving the target increase in social media followers and engagement metrics.

Content Moderation Team

- **Objective Metrics:**
  - Timeliness and effectiveness of content moderation.
- **Pay Grade and Bonus:**
  - Base salary + bonus tied to maintaining a high standard of content moderation and minimizing user complaints.

Overall Performance Evaluation and Bonus Allocation

o *Regular performance evaluations should be conducted based on the established metrics for each position.*

o *Bonuses should be awarded based on achieving or exceeding the predetermined targets.*

o *The bonus structure can be a percentage of the base salary, with higher percentages awarded for exceptional performance.*

By aligning pay grades and bonuses with each position's standards of performance, the newspaper can incentivize employees to strive for excellence and contribute to the overall success of the organization in reaching its goal of 60,000 transactions per month.[§]

Summary

The execution stage of the MVOSSTE process requires that the workforce has a plan, a structure, a process for describing jobs for individuals, and controls that measure how well jobs are done.

The planning, organizing, directing, and controlling of the workforce must be built around the overall organization's mission, vision, objective, strategy, and tactics.

Cash Requirements

Planning

A plan for cash requirements must identify the sources of cash, the uses for cash, and how cash might be used to invest in the organization for growth. Using AI to create a cash management plan can be helpful and for the newspaper example might look like:

[§]ChatGPT resending to the prompt "For a newspaper with a monthly expense budget of $500,000, trying to reach 18 to 30-year-old social media users, using the set of tactics for the workforce needed to have a successful organization generating 60,000 transactions per month, Create metrics that establishes pay grades and bonuses that tie to each position's standards of performance."

Managing cash effectively is crucial for the financial health and growth of a newspaper targeting 18 to 30-year-old social media users. Here are the cash systems needed to handle various aspects, considering the set of workforce tactics for a successful organization generating 60,000 transactions per month:

Collecting Cash From Subscribers and Advertisers

- *Subscription Payment System:*
  - ○ *Implement a secure and user-friendly online payment system for subscription fees.*
  - ○ *Use payment gateways to accept various payment methods, including credit/debit cards and digital wallets.*
  - ○ *Utilize subscription management software to automate recurring billing and track subscription payments.*
- *Ad Revenue Collection System:*
  - ○ *Set up an efficient system for collecting advertising revenue from advertisers.*
  - ○ *Offer multiple payment options and establish clear invoicing processes.*
  - ○ *Utilize ad management platforms that streamline the payment process and provide detailed billing information.*

Allocating Cash

- *Budgeting Software:*
  - ○ *Implement budgeting software to allocate cash effectively across different departments and initiatives.*
  - ○ *Establish clear budget categories for workforce expenses, content creation, marketing, and technology upgrades.*
  - ○ *Regularly review and adjust budget allocations based on performance metrics and organizational priorities.*
- *Financial Management Tools:*
  - ○ *Utilize financial management tools to track expenses in real time.*

- ○ *Categorize expenditures, allowing for a transparent view of cash allocation across various functions.*
- ○ *Generate financial reports for comprehensive insights into spending patterns.*

Paying Bills

- **Accounts Payable System:**
  - ○ *Implement an accounts payable system to manage and pay bills efficiently.*
  - ○ *Streamline the invoice approval process and establish payment schedules.*
  - ○ *Utilize electronic payment methods to ensure timely and secure transactions.*
- **Expense Approval Workflow:**
  - ○ *Set up an expense approval workflow that involves relevant stakeholders.*
  - ○ *Implement spending controls and ensure adherence to budgetary guidelines.*
  - ○ *Integrate expense tracking tools with budgeting software for seamless financial management.*

Investing in Growth

- **Financial Planning for Growth:**
  - ○ *Develop a financial growth plan that outlines investment opportunities.*
  - ○ *Allocate a portion of the budget for strategic investments in technology upgrades, marketing campaigns, and talent acquisition.*
- **Capital Expenditure Planning:**
  - ○ *Identify key areas for capital expenditure that align with organizational goals.*
  - ○ *Allocate funds for technology infrastructure, platform enhancements, and other growth-related initiatives.*
- **Financial Analysis and Projections:**

    ○ *Conduct financial analysis and projections to assess the potential return on investment.*

    ○ *Regularly review financial performance against growth objectives to make informed investment decisions.*

Overall Cash Management Considerations

- **Cash Flow Forecasting**
  - ○ *Implement cash flow forecasting tools to anticipate future cash needs.*
  - ○ *Adjust spending and investment plans based on forecasted cash flows.*
- **Financial Audits**
  - ○ *Conduct periodic financial audits to ensure transparency and compliance.*
  - ○ *Utilize audit findings to enhance financial management practices.*
- **Emergency Fund**
  - ○ *Maintain an emergency fund to address unforeseen challenges or opportunities.*
  - ○ *Ensure that a portion of the budget is reserved for contingencies.*
- **Financial Advisory Services**
  - ○ *Consider engaging financial advisory services for expert guidance on investment decisions.*
  - ○ *Seek professional advice for optimizing cash management strategies.*

By implementing these cash systems, the newspaper can effectively collect, allocate, pay, and invest cash, supporting its growth objectives while maintaining financial stability. Regular monitoring and adjustments based on financial performance will contribute to sustained success.¶

¶ChatGPT response to the prompt "For a newspaper with a monthly expense budget of $500,000, trying to reach 18 to 30-year-old social media users, using the set of tactics for the workforce needed to have a successful organization generating 60,000 transactions per month. Identify the cash systems needed to collect cash from subscriber and advertisers, allocate cash, pay bills, and invest in the growth of the company."

Organizing

Organizing the financial components in an organization requires the strategist to align internal communications to ensure the efficient use of resources. Increasing cash inflows and scheduling outflows in a manner that increases interest income and reduces late payment penalties. An AI-generated financial organization would include:

To maximize the use of financial resources and optimize cash management for the newspaper targeting 18 to 30-year-old social media users, here are financial mechanisms and strategies:

1. **Cash Flow Forecasting**
   o *Implement robust cash flow forecasting to anticipate inflows and outflows accurately.*
   o *Identify peak cash flow periods and allocate surplus funds effectively.*

2. **Cash Inflow Optimization:**
   o *Accelerate cash inflows by incentivizing early subscription renewals through discounts or bonuses.*
   o *Offer promotional deals to encourage advertisers to prepay for ad space or commit to long-term contracts.*

3. **Cash Outflow Management:**
   o *Negotiate favorable payment terms with vendors and suppliers to extend payment deadlines without incurring penalties.*
   o *Utilize electronic payment systems to streamline bill payments and avoid late fees.*

4. **Interest Income Maximization:**
   o *Invest surplus cash in short-term interest-bearing instruments such as money market accounts or certificates of deposit.*
   o *Monitor interest rates and adjust investment strategies accordingly to maximize returns.*

5. **Debt Management:**
   o *Refinance existing debts at lower interest rates to reduce interest expenses and improve cash flow.*
   o *Consolidate debts to streamline repayment and take advantage of lower interest rates.*

6. **Expense Optimization**
   o Conduct regular expense reviews to identify cost-saving opportunities and eliminate unnecessary expenditures.
   o Implement cost-cutting measures such as energy efficiency upgrades or renegotiating service contracts.

7. **Revenue Diversification:**
   o Explore alternative revenue streams such as sponsored content, events, or subscription-based premium services to supplement advertising revenue.
   o Leverage social media platforms to monetize user engagement through sponsored posts or partnerships.

8. **Budget Monitoring and Adjustment:**
   o Monitor budget performance regularly and compare actual expenses against budgeted amounts.
   o Adjust spending priorities as needed to align with revenue projections and strategic objectives.

9. **Risk Management:**
   o Implement risk management strategies to mitigate financial risks such as currency fluctuations or market volatility.
   o Maintain adequate insurance coverage to protect against unforeseen events that could impact financial stability.

By implementing these financial mechanisms and strategies, the newspaper can maximize the use of financial resources, optimize cash management, and enhance overall financial performance while reaching its target audience and generating 60,000 transactions per month.[**]

[**]ChatGPT responding to the prompt "For a newspaper with a monthly expense budget of $500,000, trying to reach 18 to 30-year-old social media users, using the set of tactics for the workforce needed to have a successful organization generating 60,000 transactions per month. Create financial mechanisms to maximize use of financial resources including maximizing cash inflows while managing cash outflows to increase interest income, reduce late payment fees."

Directing

Each of the financial functions would fall under the financial organization and require direction and standards of performance for each position. AI-generated position and standards of performance might look like:

Here are the organizational positions and standards of performance for each financial mechanism and strategy:

Cash Flow Forecasting

Position: Financial Analyst

- ***Responsibility:*** *Develop accurate cash flow forecasts based on historical data, market trends, and business projections.*
- ***Standard for Fulfillment:*** *Provide monthly cash flow forecasts with a margin of error not exceeding 5percent.*
- ***Metric for Success:*** *Achieve a variance of less than 5 percent between forecasted and actual cash flows.*

Cash Inflow Optimization

Position: Revenue Manager

- ***Responsibility:*** *Develop strategies to accelerate cash inflows through subscription renewals and advertising commitments.*
- ***Standard for Fulfillment:*** *Increase early subscription renewals by 10 percent and secure advertising prepayments for 50 percent of annual revenue.*
- ***Metric for Success:*** *Achieve a 10 percent increase in early subscription renewals and secure advertising prepayments for 50 percent of annual revenue.*

Cash Outflow Management

Position: Accounts Payable Manager

- **Responsibility:** *Negotiate favorable payment terms with vendors and suppliers to extend payment deadlines.*
- **Standard for Fulfillment:** *Extend payment terms by an average of 15 days without incurring late fees.*
- **Metric for Success:** *Maintain a zero late fee record while extending payment terms by an average of 15 days.*

Interest Income Maximization

Position: Investment Manager

- **Responsibility:** *Invest surplus cash in short-term interest-bearing instruments to maximize returns.*
- **Standard for Fulfillment:** *Achieve an average annual return on investments of at least 5 percent.*
- **Metric for Success:** *Maintain an average annual return on investments of at least 5 percent.*

Debt Management

Position: Debt Management Specialist

- **Responsibility:** *Evaluate existing debts and refinance at lower interest rates if beneficial.*
- **Standard for Fulfillment:** *Refinance at least 50 percent of existing debts at lower interest rates within one year.*
- **Metric for Success:** *Refinance at least 50 percent of existing debts at lower interest rates within one year.*

Expense Optimization

Position: Expense Analyst

- **Responsibility:** *Conduct regular expense reviews and identify cost-saving opportunities.*

- *Standard for Fulfillment:* Implement cost-saving measures resulting in a 10 percent reduction in discretionary expenses.
- *Metric for Success:* Achieve a 10 percent reduction in discretionary expenses within six months.

Revenue Diversification

Position: Revenue Diversification Manager

- *Responsibility:* Explore alternative revenue streams and develop strategies for revenue diversification.
- *Standard for Fulfillment:* Launch two new revenue-generating initiatives within the fiscal year.
- *Metric for Success:* Launch two new revenue-generating initiatives within the fiscal year.

Budget Monitoring and Adjustment

Position: Budget Analyst

- *Responsibility:* Monitor budget performance and make adjustments as needed to align with revenue projections.
- *Standard for Fulfillment:* Maintain actual expenses within 95 percent of the budgeted amounts.
- *Metric for Success:* Maintain actual expenses within 95 percent of the budgeted amounts.

Risk Management

Position: Risk Manager

- *Responsibility:* Identify and mitigate financial risks such as currency fluctuations and market volatility.
- *Standard for Fulfillment:* Develop and implement risk management strategies reducing financial risks by 20 percent.
- *Metric for Success:* Reduce financial risks by 20 percent through the implementation of risk management strategies.

By establishing clear organizational positions and standards of performance for each financial mechanism and strategy, the newspaper can effectively manage its financial resources and achieve its business objectives while reaching its target audience and generating 60,000 transactions per month.[††]

Controlling

Once the organization and mechanisms are in place, there should be a set of metrics established to measure the success of each financial position. KPIs for each financial function might look like:

Below are the KPIs for each financial function:

Financial Analyst

KPIs

- *Cash Flow Forecast Accuracy: Measure the variance between forecasted and actual cash flows.*
- *Timeliness of Reporting: Track the adherence to deadlines for submitting financial reports.*

Revenue Manager

KPIs

- *Early Subscription Renewal Rate: Percentage of subscribers renewing their subscriptions early.*
- *Advertising Prepayment Percentage: Proportion of advertising revenue received as prepayments.*

[††]ChatGPT responding to the prompt "Create organizational positions and standards of performance for each of the financial mechanisms and strategies."

Accounts Payable Manager

KPIs

- *Payment Terms Extension Rate: Percentage of vendors with extended payment terms.*
- *Late Payment Frequency: Frequency of late payments to vendors.*

Investment Manager

KPIs

- *Return on Investments (ROI): Average annual return on investment portfolio.*
- *Investment Diversification: Measure the diversification of investment portfolio across different asset classes.*

Debt Management Specialist

KPIs

- *Debt Refinancing Rate: Percentage of debts successfully refinanced at lower interest rates.*
- *Debt-to-Equity Ratio: Measure the ratio of debt to equity to assess financial leverage.*

Expense Analyst

KPIs

- *Expense Reduction Rate: Percentage reduction in discretionary expenses.*
- *Cost per Transaction: Measure the cost incurred per transaction generated.*

Revenue Diversification Manager

KPIs

- *New Revenue Initiative Launch Rate: Number of new revenue-generating initiatives launched within a specific period.*
- *Revenue Contribution From New Initiatives: Percentage of total revenue generated by new initiatives.*

Budget Analyst

KPIs

- *Budget Variance Rate: Percentage variance between actual expenses and budgeted amounts.*

- *Budget Compliance: Measure the adherence to budgeted expenses.*

Risk Manager

KPIs

- *Risk Mitigation Effectiveness: Measure the effectiveness of risk management strategies in reducing financial risks.*
- *Risk Exposure Reduction: Percentage reduction in identified financial risks over time.*

These KPIs provide measurable indicators of performance for each financial function, enabling the organization to track progress, identify areas for improvement, and make informed decisions to achieve its financial objectives.[‡‡]

[‡‡]ChatGPT responding to the prompt "Create key performance indicators for each financial function."

Operating Procedures

Planning

Operating procedures refer to the methods that individuals in the organization utilize to achieve the organization's goals. The procedures must be in line with the mission and vision and focus on providing the best outcomes for the organization. Using AI can potentially provide a more complete list of operating procedures than an individual or group of individuals since it draws from a larger dataset.

Here are some AI-generated operating procedures that might be considered.

Let's outline operating procedures for the entire organization, including editorial content positions, that tie to the standards of performance and will provide the best outcomes for reaching 18 to 30-year-old social media users and generating 60,000 transactions per month:

Editorial Content Creation

- ***Content Planning:***
  - *Develop a monthly editorial calendar outlining content themes and topics aligned with audience interests and engagement objectives.*
  - *Assign editorial content based on expertise, relevance, and performance standards.*
- ***Content Creation:***
  - *Ensure content creators adhere to established editorial guidelines, including tone, style, and quality standards.*
  - *Review and approve content submissions to ensure alignment with editorial standards and performance objectives.*
- ***Audience Engagement:***
  - *Monitor audience feedback and engagement metrics for published content.*
  - *Use insights to inform future content creation strategies and optimize audience engagement.*

Financial Management

- **_Budget Allocation:_**
  - Allocate budget resources for editorial content creation, promotion, and distribution in alignment with performance objectives.
  - Monitor expenditure against budget allocations and adjust spending as necessary to optimize resource utilization.
- **_Revenue Generation:_**
  - Develop revenue-generating opportunities through sponsored content, native advertising, and partnerships with relevant brands.
  - Track revenue performance metrics and adjust revenue strategies to meet performance targets.

Human Resources

- **_Talent Acquisition:_**
  - Recruit content creators with expertise in topics relevant to the target audience and performance objectives.
  - Conduct regular performance evaluations and provide feedback to support continuous improvement and alignment with performance standards.
- **_Training and Development:_**
  - Provide training and development opportunities to enhance content creation skills and knowledge of emerging trends in digital media and social media engagement.
  - Support ongoing learning and skill development to ensure content creators are equipped to meet performance objectives.

Operations

- **_Workflow Management:_**
  - Establish efficient workflow processes for content creation, review, and publication to ensure timely delivery and alignment with performance objectives.

- o   *Implement project management tools to track content creation progress and identify potential bottlenecks or delays.*
- **Quality Assurance:**
  - o   *Conduct regular quality assessments of published content to ensure accuracy, relevance, and adherence to performance standards.*
  - o   *Solicit feedback from audience members and stakeholders to identify areas for improvement and optimize content quality.*

Marketing and Promotion

- **Content Promotion:**
  - o   *Develop promotion strategies to increase visibility and engagement with editorial content among the target audience.*
  - o   *Utilize social media platforms and digital marketing channels to amplify content reach and drive audience engagement.*
- **Audience Growth:**
  - o   *Implement audience growth strategies to expand reach and attract new readers within the 18 to 30-year-old demographic.*
  - o   *Analyze audience demographics and engagement metrics to refine targeting and optimize promotional efforts.*

Risk Management

- **Content Compliance:**
  - o   *Ensure editorial content complies with legal and ethical guidelines, including copyright laws, privacy regulations, and community standards.*
  - o   *Conduct regular content audits to identify and mitigate potential risks related to accuracy, credibility, and sensitivity.*
- **Crisis Management:**
  - o   *Develop crisis communication protocols to address any issues or controversies related to published content promptly and transparently.*
  - o   *Monitor social media channels and online communities for emerging issues and proactively manage reputation risks.*

By implementing these operating procedures, the newspaper organization can effectively manage editorial content creation, financial resources, human resources, operations, marketing, and risk management functions to achieve the best outcomes for reaching 18 to 30-year-old social media users and generating 60,000 transactions per month.[§§]

Organizing

Organizing operating procedures so they are in alignment with workforce, cash requirements, and fixed asset deployment will ensure that all components of the organization are supporting the same goals that will provide a successful operation for the organization.

To optimize the operating procedures and align them with the workforce tactics for reaching 18 to 30-year-old social media users and generating 60,000 transactions per month, let's create an organizational structure for the newspaper:

Organizational Structure

Editorial Department

- ***Editor-in-Chief:*** *Oversees editorial content strategy, quality control, and audience engagement.*
- ***Content Editors:*** *Manage content planning, creation, and publication processes.*
- ***Journalists/Content Creators:*** *Produce engaging and relevant content tailored to the target audience.*
- ***Social Media Managers:*** *Develop and execute social media strategies to promote editorial content and engage with the audience.*

[§§]ChatGPT responding to the prompt "For a newspaper with a monthly expense budget of $500,000, trying to reach 18 to 30-year-old social media users, using the set of tactics for the workforce needed to have a successful organization generating 60,000 transactions per month. Create operating procedures for the entire organization including the editorial content positions that tie to the standards of performance and will provide the best outcomes for the organization."

Financial Management Department

- ***Chief Financial Officer (CFO):*** *Responsible for budget allocation, financial planning, and revenue generation strategies.*
- ***Financial Analysts:*** *Monitor and analyze financial performance metrics, track budget adherence, and provide insights for decision making.*
- ***Revenue Managers:*** *Develop and implement revenue-generating initiatives, such as advertising partnerships and sponsored content opportunities.*
- ***Accounts Payable/Receivable:*** *Manage vendor payments, invoicing, and revenue collection processes.*

Human Resources Department

- ***Human Resources Director:*** *Leads talent acquisition, training, performance management, and workforce planning efforts.*
- ***Recruiters:*** *Source and recruit talent aligned with the organization's objectives and target audience requirements.*
- ***Training and Development Specialists:*** *Design and deliver training programs to enhance employee skills and knowledge.*
- ***HR Generalists:*** *Handle day-to-day HR operations, employee relations, and compliance matters.*

Operations Department

- ***Operations Manager:*** *Oversees operational processes, workflow optimization, and quality assurance initiatives.*
- ***Project Managers:*** *Coordinate content production schedules, track project milestones, and ensure timely delivery.*
- ***Quality Assurance Specialists:*** *Conduct content audits, monitor performance metrics, and implement quality improvement measures.*
- ***IT Support:*** *Provide technical support, maintain digital infrastructure, and ensure system reliability and security.*

Marketing and Promotion Department

- ***Chief Marketing Officer (CMO):*** *Develops and executes marketing strategies to promote content and grow audience engagement.*
- ***Marketing Managers:*** *Plan and implement marketing campaigns across various channels, including social media, e-mail, and digital advertising.*
- ***Social Media Specialists:*** *Manage social media platforms, create engaging content, and interact with followers to drive audience growth and engagement.*
- ***Promotions Coordinators:*** *Coordinate promotional offers, events, and partnerships to attract new readers and retain existing subscribers.*

Risk Management Department

- ***Risk Manager:*** *Identifies, assesses, and mitigates potential risks related to content, financial operations, and reputation.*
- ***Legal Counsel:*** *Provides legal guidance on content compliance, contracts, intellectual property, and regulatory compliance.*
- ***Crisis Communication Team:*** *Develops and implements crisis communication plans to address reputational risks and manage public relations during emergencies.*

Conclusion

*This organizational structure optimizes the operating procedures by aligning each department and role with specific functions and objectives aimed at reaching the target audience, driving engagement, and achieving revenue goals within the allocated budget. Effective collaboration and communication between departments are crucial for the seamless execution of strategies and achieving the organization's mission and vision.*⁵⁵

---

⁵⁵ChatGPT responding to the prompt "For a newspaper with a monthly expense budget of $500,000, trying to reach 18 to 30-year-old social media users, using the set of tactics for the workforce needed to have a successful

Directing

Operating procedures should tie to workforce requirements and job descriptions for the best outcomes. AI can help with the matching of operating procedures to workforce cash and fixed asset requirements.

Here is an AI-generated list of operating procedures that considers workforce, cash requirements, and fixed assets.

Let's integrate cash management and fixed asset components into the standards of performance for the newspaper organization targeting 18 to 30-year-old social media users and aiming to generate 60,000 transactions per month:

Editorial Department

- **Content Planning and Creation:**
  - Standard: Develop an editorial calendar with at least 80 percent of content aligned with audience interests and engagement objectives.
  - Metric: Measure content relevance and engagement through social media shares, comments, and page views. Aim for a monthly increase of 10 percent in engagement metrics.

- **Quality Assurance:**
  - Standard: Ensure 95 percent of published content meets editorial guidelines for accuracy, relevance, and tone.
  - Metric: Conduct monthly content audits and maintain a 90 percent or higher quality rating based on editorial assessments.
- **Cash Management:**
  - Standard: Maintain a cash reserve equivalent to 10 percent of the monthly budget for operational contingencies.
  - Metric: Monitor cash reserves and adjust cash management strategies to optimize liquidity while minimizing idle cash.
- **Fixed Assets Management:**

---

organization generating 60,000 transactions per month. Create an organizational structure that optimizes the operating procedures created."

o *Standard: Ensure proper maintenance and utilization of fixed assets to minimize downtime and maximize operational efficiency.*

o *Metric: Conduct regular assessments of fixed assets' condition and performance to identify maintenance needs and optimize asset utilization.*

Financial Management Department

- **Budget Allocation:**
  o *Standard: Allocate budget resources according to approved plans with less than 5 percent deviation from budgeted amounts.*
  o *Metric: Monitor budget variance and adjust allocations as needed to ensure adherence to financial targets.*
- **Revenue Generation:**
  o *Standard: Achieve a monthly revenue increase of at least 10 percent through advertising partnerships and sponsored content.*
  o *Metric: Track revenue performance against targets and implement revenue enhancement strategies to meet or exceed goals.*
- **Cash Flow Management:**
  o *Standard: Maintain positive cash flow and minimize reliance on external financing to fund operations.*
  o *Metric: Monitor cash flow metrics such as cash conversion cycle and cash-to-cash cycle time to optimize cash flow efficiency.*

Human Resources Department

- **Talent Acquisition:**
  o *Standard: Fill vacant positions within 60 days of approval with candidates meeting 80 percent or more of required qualifications.*
  o *Metric: Monitor time-to-hire and candidate quality to ensure timely recruitment of suitable talent.*
- **Training and Development:**

- o *Standard: Provide at least 20 hours of training per employee annually to enhance skills and knowledge relevant to their roles.*
- o *Metric: Measure training hours and employee feedback to assess training effectiveness and identify areas for improvement.*

Operations Department

- **Workflow Management:**
  - o *Standard: Complete content production cycles within established timelines with less than 10 percent of projects delayed.*
  - o *Metric: Monitor project milestones and identify bottlenecks to ensure timely delivery of content.*
- **Quality Assurance:**
  - o *Standard: Maintain a content quality rating of 90 percent or higher based on monthly audits and audience feedback.*
  - o *Metric: Conduct regular quality assessments and address any deviations from performance standards promptly.*

Marketing and Promotion Department

- **Content Promotion:**
  - o *Standard: Increase social media engagement metrics by 15 percent monthly through targeted content promotion strategies.*
  - o *Metric: Track engagement metrics such as likes, shares, and comments to evaluate the effectiveness of promotional efforts.*
- **Audience Growth:**
  - o *Standard: Achieve a monthly increase of 5 percent in subscriber base and social media followers within the target demographic.*
  - o *Metric: Monitor audience growth metrics and adjust marketing strategies to drive subscriber acquisition and retention.*

Conclusion

Integrating cash management and fixed asset components into the standards of performance ensures that financial resources are effectively managed to support operational objectives while optimizing the utilization of fixed assets to drive efficiency and productivity. Regular monitoring and evaluation of performance *metrics will enable the organization to maintain financial health and achieve its strategic goals.***

Controlling

Operating procedures are focused on overall organizational activity and would include workforce, cash requirements, and fixed assets. This KPIs would consider all aspects of the organization.

Here are some metrics developed by AI for operating procedures for the newspaper example.

Let's create KPIs that tie to the operating procedures, including cash management and fixed asset components, for a newspaper aiming to reach 18 to 30-year-old social media users and generate 60,000 transactions per month:

Financial Management KPIs

- **Budget Adherence:**
  - *KPI: Maintain budget variance within ± 5 percent of allocated amounts for each expense category.*
  - *Metric: Monthly comparison of actual expenses against budgeted amounts for all operational categories.*
- **Cash Flow Efficiency:**
  - *KPI: Achieve a positive cash flow of at least $50,000 per month.*
  - *Metric: Monthly comparison of cash inflows (revenue and investments) and outflows (expenses and debt repayments).*
- **Fixed Asset Utilization:**
  - *KPI: Maintain fixed asset utilization rate above 80 percent.*
  - *Metric: Monthly assessment of the percentage of time fixed assets (e.g., printing presses, office equipment) are actively used for revenue-generating activities.*

***ChatGPT responding to the prompt "For a newspaper with a monthly expense budget of $500,000, trying to reach 18 to 30-year-old social media users, using the set of tactics for the workforce needed to have a successful organization generating 60,000 transactions per month. Create standards of performance that tie to the operating procedures and include cash management and fixed asset components."

Human Resources KPIs

- **Employee Productivity:**
  - o *KPI: Maintain an average productivity rate of 90 percent across all departments.*
  - o *Metric: Quarterly review of employee output and efficiency compared to established performance targets.*
- **Turnover Rate:**
  - o *KPI: Achieve an annual turnover rate of less than 10 percent.*
  - o *Metric: Annual calculation of the percentage of employees who leave the organization voluntarily or involuntarily.*

Operations KPIs

- **Content Production Efficiency:**
  - o *KPI: Complete 95 percent of content production cycles within established timelines.*
  - o *Metric: Monthly assessment of the percentage of projects completed on schedule.*
- **Quality Assurance:**
  - o *KPI: Maintain a content quality rating of 90 percent or higher based on audience feedback.*
  - o *Metric: Quarterly review of content quality scores and audience engagement metrics.*

Marketing and Promotion KPIs

- **Audience Engagement:**
  - o *KPI: Increase social media engagement metrics by 10 percent monthly.*
  - o *Metric: Monthly tracking of likes, shares, comments, and other engagement indicators across social media platforms.*
- **Subscriber Growth:**
  - o *KPI: Achieve a monthly subscriber growth rate of 5 percent.*
  - o *Metric: Monthly comparison of new subscriber acquisitions versus churn rate.*

Risk Management KPIs

- ***Compliance Adherence:***
  - ○ *KPI: Maintain a compliance rate of 95 percent or higher with legal and regulatory requirements.*
  - ○ *Metric: Quarterly review of compliance audits and corrective actions taken.*
- ***Risk Mitigation Effectiveness:***
  - ○ *KPI: Reduce the frequency of risk incidents by 10 percent annually.*
  - ○ *Metric: Annual assessment of risk incident reports and effectiveness of mitigation strategies implemented.*

Conclusion

These KPIs are designed to align with the operating procedures and workforce tactics, ensuring that each aspect of the organization contributes effectively to its goals of reaching the target audience and generating revenue. Regular monitoring of these KPIs will provide insights into performance trends and areas for improvement, enabling the organization to optimize its operations and achieve success.[†††]

Fixed Assets

Fixed assets refer to the capital equipment required and include machinery, computer hardware, furniture, automobiles, and other assets that are useful for a long period of time and, therefore, are not generally treated as an expense in one accounting period.

[†††]ChatGPT responding to the prompt "For a newspaper with a monthly expense budget of $500,000, trying to reach 18 to 30-year-old social media users, using the set of tactics for the workforce needed to have a successful organization generating 60,000 transactions per month. Create key performance indicators that tie to the operating procedures and include cash management and fixed asset components."

Planning

Planning for fixed assets requires an understanding of the organization's size and production requirements as well as the most efficient means of acquiring the assets.

Again, AI can provide a list of options for the organization to consider. Here is a list of fixed assets that might be needed. Note that AI is suggesting a printing press. The organization might already have a press since it is a newspaper seeking to attract 18 to 30-year-old social media users.

To determine the fixed assets required for a newspaper targeting 18 to 30-year-old social media users and generating 60,000 transactions per month, considering the identified workforce and operating procedures, we can identify the following fixed assets:

- ***Printing Equipment:***
  - *Offset printing press*
  - *Digital printing equipment*
- ***Office Equipment:***
  - *Computers/laptops*
  - *Printers and scanners*
  - *Office furniture (desks, chairs, cabinets)*
- ***Content Creation Tools:***
  - *Graphic design software (Adobe Creative Suite, Canva)*
  - Video editing software (Adobe Premiere Pro, Final Cut Pro)
  - *Content management system (CMS) for publishing*
- ***Social Media Management Tools:***
  - *Social media scheduling and analytics platforms (Hootsuite, Buffer)*
  - *Audience engagement tools (Sprout Social, HubSpot)*
- ***Communication Tools:***
  - *E-mail marketing software (Mailchimp, Constant Contact)*
  - *Internal communication tools (Slack, Microsoft Teams)*
- ***Security Systems:***
  - *Cybersecurity software and tools (firewalls, antivirus software)*
  - *Physical security equipment (security cameras, access control systems)*

- *Distribution Vehicles:*
  - Delivery vans or trucks for physical newspaper distribution
  - Digital content delivery platforms (website hosting, content delivery networks)

Acquisition of Fixed Assets

The most efficient means of acquiring these fixed assets can vary depending on factors such as budget, operational needs, and availability. Here are some options to consider:

- *Purchase:*
  - Buying new or used equipment outright with cash or financing.
- *Lease:*
  - Leasing equipment allows for flexibility and lower upfront costs. It also provides the option to upgrade to newer equipment when needed.
- *Outsourcing:*
  - Contracting with third-party vendors for services like printing and distribution can eliminate the need for purchasing certain fixed assets.
- *Subscription Services:*
  - Subscribing to software-as-a-service (SaaS) platforms for content creation, social media management, and communication tools can provide access to necessary resources without large upfront costs.
- *Asset Sharing:*
  - Collaborating with other organizations or media outlets to share certain fixed assets, such as printing equipment or distribution vehicles, can reduce individual ownership and maintenance costs.

By carefully assessing the operational needs and budget constraints, the newspaper can determine the most efficient and cost-effective means of acquiring the required fixed assets to support its workforce and operations.[‡‡‡]

[‡‡‡]ChatGPT responding to the prompt "For a newspaper with a monthly expense budget of $500,000, trying to reach 18 to 30-year-old social media users, using the set of tactics for the workforce needed to have a successful organization generating

Organizing

Fixed assets should be arranged in a fashion that ensures the most efficient use of resources and the optimal organizational output. Here is an AI-generated suggested fixed asset setup that would potentially provide best outcomes. Note the printing press was not considered in this structure.

To maximize operational efficiency and workflows for a newspaper targeting 18 to 30-year-old social media users and relying solely on digital platforms, the fixed assets can be arranged in a manner that facilitates seamless content creation, management, and distribution. Here's a suggested arrangement:

- ***Centralized Content Creation Hub:***
  - o *High-performance computers/laptops equipped with necessary software tools (Adobe Creative Suite, video editing software) for content creation.*
  - o *Dedicated workspace for content creators equipped with ergonomic furniture and proper lighting.*
- ***Content Management System (CMS):***
  - o *Centralized CMS platform for content storage, organization, and publication.*
  - o *Accessible to all content creators, editors, and managers for streamlined collaboration and workflow management.*
- ***Digital Asset Library:***
  - o *Cloud-based storage solution for storing multimedia assets (images, videos, graphics).*
  - o *Organized folder structure and metadata tagging system for easy retrieval and reuse of assets.*
- ***Social Media Management Hub:***
  - o *Integrated social media management platform (Hootsuite, Buffer) for scheduling, monitoring, and analyzing social media content.*

60,000 transactions per month, identify the fixed assets that will be required considering the workforce that has been identified. Also include the most efficient means of acquiring those fixed assets."

- Connected to the CMS for seamless content distribution across multiple social media channels.
- **E-mail Marketing Platform:**
  - Dedicated e-mail marketing software (Mailchimp, Constant Contact) for managing subscriber lists, creating e-mail campaigns, and tracking performance metrics.
  - Integration with the CMS for automated e-mail notifications and newsletters.
- **Website Hosting and Domain:**
  - Secure website hosting service with robust infrastructure and uptime guarantees.
  - Domain registration with reliable domain registrar for brand identity and online presence.
- **Digital Advertising Platforms:**
  - Access to digital advertising platforms (Google Ads, Facebook Ads) for monetizing digital content through targeted advertisements.
  - Integration with analytics tools for tracking ad performance and optimizing ad campaigns.
- **Collaborative Communication Tools:**
  - Instant messaging platforms (Slack, Microsoft Teams) for real-time communication and collaboration among team members.
  - Video conferencing software for remote meetings and brainstorming sessions.

By arranging fixed assets in this manner, the newspaper can streamline its operational workflows, promote collaboration among team members, and ensure efficient content creation, distribution, and audience engagement across digital platforms. Additionally, integrating these assets allows for seamless data exchange and workflow automation, further enhancing operational efficiency and productivity.[§§§]

[§§§]ChatGPT responding to the prompt "Arrange the fixed assets in a manner that maximizes operational efficiency and workflows."

Directing

Directing for fixed assets is related to identifying the optimum use for the fixed assets and tying these to standards of performance. An AI-generated set of standards for the use of fixed assets could look like:

Here are some standards of performance for the use of fixed assets tied to workforce positions:

- **Content Creators:**
  - ○ *Standard: Produce a minimum of five high-quality articles/videos/graphics per week.*
  - ○ *Metric: Number of published content pieces meeting editorial standards within the specified time frame.*
- **Editors:**
  - ○ *Standard: Review and edit a minimum of 10 content pieces per day for accuracy, clarity, and adherence to style guidelines.*
  - ○ *Metric: Percentage of content pieces meeting editorial standards after review.*
- **Social Media Managers:**
  - ○ *Standard: Schedule and publish a minimum of three social media posts per day across all platforms.*
  - ○ *Metric: Engagement metrics (likes, shares, comments) and click-through rates for social media posts.*
- **E-mail Marketers:**
  - ○ *Standard: Send out a weekly newsletter featuring curated content and promotional offers.*
  - ○ *Metric: Open rates, click-through rates, and subscriber growth for e-mail campaigns.*
- **Website Administrators:**
  - ○ *Standard: Ensure website uptime of 99.9 percent and resolve any technical issues within 24 hours.*
  - ○ *Metric: Downtime percentage and average time to resolution for website-related issues.*
- **Advertising Managers:**

○   *Standard: Optimize ad campaigns to achieve a minimum click-through rate (CTR) of 2 percent.*

○   *Metric: Ad performance metrics (CTR, conversion rate, return on ad spend) compared to industry benchmarks.*

- **IT Support Staff:**
  ○   *Standard: Provide timely technical support and troubleshooting assistance to resolve user issues within one hour.*

  ○   *Metric: Average response time and resolution time for IT support tickets.*

- **Collaborative Communication:**
  ○   *Standard: Maintain active participation in team communication channels, responding to messages and queries promptly.*

  ○   *Metric: Frequency of participation in team discussions and responsiveness to communication.*

These standards of performance provide clear expectations for each workforce position regarding the utilization of fixed assets to achieve organizational goals. Regular monitoring and feedback can help ensure adherence to these standards and identify areas for improvement in asset utilization and workflow efficiency.⁅⁅⁅

Controlling

Controls for fixed assets rely on KPIs that assure efficient use of the assets. Here is an AI-generated list of potential KPIs.

Here are KPIs that would promote optimal efficacy of the fixed assets:

- **Content Creation Efficiency:**
  ○   *KPI: Average time taken to produce and publish a piece of content.*

  ○   *Metric: Time elapsed from content ideation to publication, measured in hours or days.*

- **Content Quality:**

⁅⁅⁅ChatGPT responding to the prompt "Create standards of performance for the use of the fixed assets and tie to the workforce positions."

- o   *KPI: Content engagement and satisfaction metrics.*
- o   *Metric: Average engagement rates (likes, shares, comments) and audience feedback ratings for published content.*
- **Asset Utilization:**
  - o   *KPI: Utilization rate of digital assets and tools.*
  - o   *Metric: Percentage of time fixed assets (software tools, computers) are actively used for productive tasks.*
- **Social Media Reach:**
  - o   *KPI: Growth in social media followers and reach.*
  - o   *Metric: Percentage increase in followers, impressions, and reach across social media platforms.*
- **E-mail Marketing Effectiveness:**
  - o   *KPI: E-mail open rates and click-through rates.*
  - o   *Metric: Average open rate and click-through rate for e-mail campaigns compared to industry benchmarks.*
- **Website Performance:**
  - o   *KPI: Website uptime and page load speed.*
  - o   *Metric: Percentage of uptime and average page load time, measured regularly to ensure optimal performance.*
- **Ad Campaign ROI:**
  - o   *KPI: Return on investment (ROI) for digital advertising campaigns.*
  - o   *Metric: Ratio of revenue generated to advertising spend, calculated for each campaign.*
- **IT Support Responsiveness:**
  - o   *KPI: Average response time and resolution time for IT support tickets.*
  - o   *Metric: Time taken to acknowledge, respond, and resolve user-reported issues with fixed assets.*
- **Collaborative Communication Effectiveness:**
  - o   *KPI: Team communication and collaboration metrics.*
  - o   *Metric: Frequency of communication, participation in team discussions, and alignment on project goals.*
- **Cost Efficiency:**
  - o   *KPI: Cost per transaction or cost per acquisition.*

   o *Metric: Total expenses incurred divided by the number of transactions or acquisitions, aiming for continuous improvement in cost efficiency.*

 By monitoring these KPIs regularly, the organization can assess the performance and effectiveness of its fixed assets, identify areas for improvement, and make data-driven decisions to optimize asset utilization and operational efficiency.[****]

Summary

After a strategy and tactics have been identified, an execution plan is necessary to ensure that the workforce, cash requirements, operating procedures, and fixed assets work in concert to ensure overall organizational success.

AI can be helpful in generating suggested lists of ways to plan, organize, direct, and control the workforce, cash requirements, operating procedures, and fixed assets. These lists may be incomplete and in all cases must be reviewed to ensure they support organizational goals.

Having assembled the mission, vision, research-based strategy, tactics, and plan for execution, the strategists must review them carefully to ensure they are in alignment and all activities build toward achieving the organization's goals.

[****]ChatGPT responding to the prompt "Create key performance indicators that would promote optimal efficacy of the fixed assets"

CHAPTER 8

Conclusion

During the process of writing this book, I introduced ChatGPT to the MVOSSTE approach and throughout used prompts that tried to tie all elements together in a supportive fashion.

ChatGPT (and CoPilot) were asked to create a complete marketing strategy using the MVOSSTE approach. Here are the results.

Newspaper Organization

The newspaper organization example in this book depicted a newspaper wanting to use a Blue Ocean strategy to attract 18 to 30-year-old media users. Asking ChatGPT to create a marketing strategy and plan using the MVOSSTE approach resulted in the following output:

Certainly! Let's break down the marketing strategy and plan for the newspaper targeting 18 to 30-year-old social media users using the MVOSSTE approach, including price, place, product, and promotion strategies, as well as budget allocation, job descriptions, standards of performance, and key performance indicators (KPIs) for each aspect:

Mission (M)

Mission Statement

Empowering the younger generation with engaging, relevant, and informative content, our newspaper seeks to redefine the traditional media landscape by seamlessly integrating trusted journalism with dynamic social media interactions. Our mission is to inspire, inform, and connect young adults through a blend of quality journalism and interactive digital experiences, fostering a more informed and engaged community.

Vision (V)

Vision Statement

To become the leading digital media platform for young adults, offering a diverse range of content that entertains, educates, and empowers, while fostering meaningful connections and dialogue among our audience.

Objectives (O)

- **One-Year Objective:**
  - Increase monthly transactions to 60,000 through targeted social media campaigns and content optimization.
  - Grow social media following by 20 percent within the first year.
  - Achieve a 10 percent increase in subscriber base through promotional offers and engaging content.
- **Five-Year Objective:**
  - Establish ourselves as the go-to digital news source for young adults, with a monthly transaction rate of over 100,000.
  - Expand into new content verticals, such as lifestyle, technology, and entertainment, to cater to diverse interests.
  - Develop strategic partnerships with brands and influencers to enhance brand visibility and reach.

Strategies (S)

- *Product Strategy:*
  - Offer a mix of news, lifestyle, entertainment, and interactive content tailored to the interests of 18 to 30-year-old social media users.
  - Develop a user-friendly digital platform with intuitive navigation and personalized content recommendations.
- *Price Strategy:*
  - Offer tiered subscription plans with varying levels of access and benefits to cater to different user preferences.
  - Implement competitive pricing strategies to attract price-sensitive users while maintaining profitability.

- *Place Strategy:*
  - o *Focus on digital distribution channels, including website, mobile app, and social media platforms, to reach the target audience where they spend most of their time.*
  - o *Explore partnerships with popular social media influencers and online communities to extend reach and engagement.*
- *Promotion Strategy:*
  - o *Utilize targeted digital advertising campaigns on social media platforms to raise brand awareness and drive user acquisition.*
  - o *Leverage influencer marketing and user-generated content to amplify promotional efforts and foster community engagement.*

Structure (S)

- *Budget Allocation:*
  - o *Content Development: $150,000/year*
  - o *Social Media Marketing: $100,000/year*
  - o *Audience Acquisition: $100,000/year*
  - o *Partnerships and Collaborations: $50,000/year*
  - o *IT and Infrastructure: $50,000/year*
  - o *Miscellaneous Expenses: $50,000/year*

Tactics (T)

- *Content Development:*
  - o *Job Descriptions: Content creators, editors.*
  - o *Standards of Performance: Publish X number of articles/videos per week, maintain editorial quality standards.*
  - o *KPIs: Content engagement metrics, subscriber growth rate.*
- *Social Media Marketing:*
  - o *Job Descriptions: Social media managers, marketing specialists.*
  - o *Standards of Performance: Increase follower base by X percent, achieve X percent engagement rate on posts.*
  - o *KPIs: Social media engagement metrics, follower growth rate.*
- *Audience Acquisition:*
  - o *Job Descriptions: Marketing specialists, e-mail marketers.*

- o   *Standards of Performance: Achieve X percent conversion rate from advertising campaigns, grow subscriber base by X percent.*
- o   *KPIs: Conversion rate, subscriber growth rate.*
- *Partnerships and Collaborations:*
  - o   *Job Descriptions: Chief marketing officer, marketing specialists.*
  - o   *Standards of Performance: Secure X number of partnerships, measure ROI from collaboration initiatives.*
  - o   *KPIs: Number of partnerships secured, ROI from collaborations.*

Execution (E)

- **Key Performance Indicators (KPIs):**
  - o   *Monthly Transaction Volume*
  - o   *Social Media Engagement Metrics (likes, shares, comments)*
  - o   *Subscriber Growth Rate*
  - o   *E-mail Open Rates and Click-Through Rates*
  - o   *ROI From Advertising Campaigns*
  - o   *Number of Strategic Partnerships Secured*

Regular monitoring of these KPIs will allow for ongoing evaluation of the effectiveness of the marketing strategies and tactics, enabling adjustments and optimizations as needed to achieve organizational objectives. [*]

While this is a pretty good start, it is not a robust marketing strategy and plan but it does provide a skeleton that can be fleshed out by some good marketing strategists and executives.

Please note that it assumed research or Situation Analysis was not needed and replaced Situation analysis with Structure. This is a good indication of why the marketing strategist should go through each

---

[*]ChatGPT responding to two prompts "For a newspaper with a monthly expense budget of $500,000, trying to reach 18 to 30-year-old social media users, a Blue Ocean strategy approach to have a successful organization generating 60,000 transactions per month, create a full marketing strategy and plan using the MVOSSTE approach, include price, place, product, and promotion strategies, include budget for each department in the total organization, job descriptions, standards of performance and key performance indicators for the workforce, cash requirements, operating procedures, and fixed assets," and "provide budget for each department in the total organization, job descriptions, standards of performance and key performance indicators for the workforce, cash requirements, operating procedures and fixed assets."

MVOSSTE step before proceeding to the next. In this case the research phase might have uncovered additional steps or identified unacceptable approaches.

Summary

The key to developing a complete marketing strategy and plan is to remember to incorporate mission, vision, objective, situation analysis, strategy (the 4Ps creating value for the 3Cs), tactics, and execution. If AI is used at each stage of the MVOSSTE process, the strategists will need to ensure that each successive phase is in sync with the previous stage. Along the way, each stage must be assessed as to its fit with the organization, its culture, its resources, and its objectives. Using AI, while not the complete answer, provides the marketing strategists and planners a large selection of options to consider at each stage of the MVOSSTE process.

While many executives have used similar approaches to create or restructure businesses, they may find it useful to use a structured approach like MVOSSTE and use generative AI to get a more robust set of options and ideas.

Notes

Chapter 1

1. Coca Cola (2020).
2. Levitt (1975).
3. Christensen (2003).

Chapter 2

1. Coca Cola (2020).

Chapter 5

1. Randazzo (2014), pp. 56–57.

References

Christensen, C. 2003. In *The Innovator's Solution*. Cambridge, MA: Harvard Business Press.

Coca Cola. (2020). "Mission, Vision and Values." coca-cola.com, (accessed October 2, 2024).Ibid.

Randazzo, G. 2014. In *Developing Successful Marketing Strategies*. Business Expert Press, 56–57.

Levitt, T. September–October 1975. In *Marketing Myopia*. Harvard Business Review.

About the Author

Gary W. Randazzo, MBA, is a senior professor of practice at the University of Houston C.T. Bauer College of Business and teaches a business consulting lab for MBA students. Students in this class work with real companies and address current challenges facing those clients. Projects range from marketing strategies for multinational banks to operational systems design for resource allocation by a major airport system to location strategies for small service businesses. Mr. Randazzo also teaches undergraduate classes in marketing strategy and planning.

Mr. Randazzo is also president of GWR Research, a management and marketing consulting firm, has served as CEO, CFO, and CIO of large and small companies, and has been a partner and founder of several startups. While most firms are domestic, Mr. Randazzo served as chairman of an international LED sign company. Mr. Randazzo also served as Senior Vice President of the Houston Chronicle and Executive Vice President and General Manager of the San Francisco Chronicle.

Mr. Randazzo has served as Chairman of Leadership Houston, Chairman of Big Brother Big Sisters of Southeast Texas, and Vice President of the Kiwanis Club of Houston. He has also served on the boards of Project Grad, the 100 Club, and is a senior fellow of the American Leadership Forum.

Mr. Randazzo is married to Sue and has four children, Daniel, Vanessa, Jason, and Gary Jr.

Index

Printed in the USA
CPSIA information can be obtained
at www.ICGtesting.com
JSHW011150101024
71158JS00011B/56

9 781637 427309